INSPIRATIONS
FROM THE PHATBOY

By
Phillip Marcha

Contents

PREFACE

Allow me to introduce myself. My given name is Phillip Marcha.

Over the years, I have gained a little weight, started riding Harley's, opened my last restaurant called PHATBOY PHIL'S, and now I'm trying to slip into retirement. My experiences, jobs, friends, travels, and my recent medical issues have inspired me from time to time. Call it divine intervention, too much whiskey, or just too much time on my hands...these inspirations usually come to me when its quiet, and I am alone.

I discovered my knack for writing around the 7th or 8th grade, thanks to my middle school English teachers and my first Speech teacher. Although I received a few well-deserved paddling's, I went on to achieve all As in their classes and, with one of those teachers, a lifelong friendship. Nothing like English teachers with a paddle in their hands to drive home grammar and comp!!!

Although I was more interested in girls and sports, the influence of my teachers planted a seed that long sat dormant. It has only taken 50 years to come to fruition.

I wrote my first piece, COMING FULL CIRCLE, in 2013 after attending the 73rd Sturgis bike rally (Harley's 110th anniversary). I rode 912 miles to Sturgis and over 2000 by the time I got back to my hometown Altus, Oklahoma, a town of about 20k. The ride gave me plenty of time to reflect on my life and write. I gave a copy to my parents for Christmas, and my mother framed it with her stamp of approval. I was content with writing just that one piece.

But in August 2015, myself and six other biker buddies of mine, took off for Sturgis again. As it was the 75th Sturgis rally, and I was about to get married for the second time, I had more time to reflect on my life and my future.

Now knowing that three days later, I would be getting married once again; to say I was a bit anxious would be an understatement. April, my current wife of nine years, and I were to get married, in Hog Heaven, by my pledge brother Pastor Paul, with him, back in Oklahoma, performing the ceremony via the phone. Tell me I am not romantic!

We took off on an extremely hot day in my hometown of Altus and ended up the first night in Vega Texas, a small town west of Amarillo. We woke up to an "Amarillo Morning" and headed west to Santa Fe, Angel Fire, and ended up in Durango. The next day we rode the Million Dollar Highway, had some cold beers in Grand Junction and ended up in Jackson Hole Wyoming where we froze our asses off. The following day we rode the Grand Tetons and Yellowstone and ended up in Casper Wyoming. I had developed bike issues coming out of Yellowstone and could only do 35 to 40 mph, so I sent the other six riders ahead. It was on this ride that I started writing LEFT HAND LOW. As we were getting close to Sturgis, the bike traffic started getting heavy. And as any biker knows, you hold your left hand out to your side when passing another biker showing respect with the greeting.

When I finally made it to Sturgis, I got my bike fixed. Then Pastor Paul married me and April in the campground. You must have priorities in life!!

Everything in my life was going great. As newlyweds, April and I were running PHATBOY PHIL'S STEAKHOUSE and

April's HIDEOUT, which was a dive bar right across the street from the steakhouse. We were having the times of our lives running two successful businesses and enjoying our friends and family. But as I entered my 60's, my health started to decline, as one usually does. Together, we reluctantly decided to fold our cards and close both businesses.

I made an appointment to see the doctor. His suggestion of getting health insurance, as I had none at the time, would prove fruitful advice. Not being a fan of public health care or government assistance to take care of me in my golden years, I researched health care options. I found that the great state of Oklahoma seemed to offer great benefits, so I went to work for the department of corrections at the state reformatory that was just across the lake that we reside on.

Now working for the DOC in food service meant feeding over 1000 medium and minimum prisoners 3 squares a day 24/7, 365 for less than $5 per prisoner a day. It was certainly a challenge despite my culinary background of close to 50 years. However, it was one of the most rewarding and gratifying experiences of my life. To be in that atmosphere amongst these men and watch them interact on a daily, truly opened my eyes. Many "inspirational" moments happened in that chow hall and later at the Wilson Gym. Observing, working with, and interacting with these men forever changed my perspective on incarcerations.

When I took my breaks or would walk my "count" up to the rotunda, I would sit very close to the condemned cells of the old prison. It was here, alone in the quiet, so close to the chair "Ol Sparky", I found time to reflect on my life compared to theirs. Once "life in the fast lane" now in the slow lane, it gave me another PHATBOY inspiration, "INSIDE LOOKING OUT, OUTSIDE LOOKING IN" was written.

After a few months of employment, I experienced a couple of brain bleeds caused by a tumor. Treatment required surgical removal of the tumor and thirty rounds of radiation. But finally, we saw the end of that medical exploration marked with "ringing the bell"; talk about perspective.

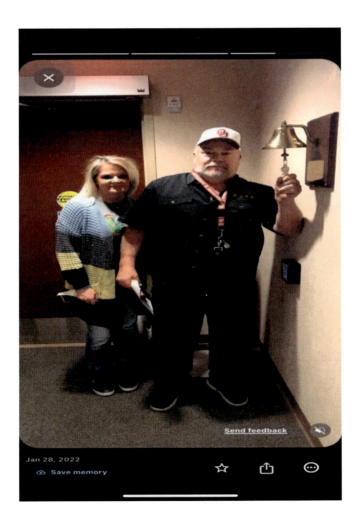

Needing to get back to work, I returned after about four weeks post-surgery. As the conditions in the chow hall were very stressful and we were running about half staffed, I asked for an internal transfer. I settled on a new and less stressful position as Correctional Activities Officer or "Coach" as the prisoners called me. My responsibilities included programing activities for adult male prisoners which at the time presented itself as ironically amusing as I hadn't yet fully understood the importance of recreation as a means of reformation. In other words, the majority of my responsibilities was to provide "recess" for over 1000 felons. Again, talk about perspective. Yet again, a disruption entered my life called "Covid" which came knocking with "lock downs" not only for the public, but inside the prison walls as well. I soon welcomed my old friend of isolation and silence. As I began to use YouTube music to fill the time, I discovered a little-known artist (at the time), Jelly Roll. A talented artist with a checkered past not to dissimilar to the same men I witnessed every day. His performance of "Simple Man" with a group called Shinedown was my introduction. It sparked my binge of his creative inspiring works. While surfing You Tube, I ran into his performance with Craig Morgan on the Grand Ol Opry stage. STANDING IN THE CIRCLE they sang "Almost Home". I still cry every time I watch this video. His crossover hit "Long Haired Son of a Sinner" inspired me to think, Hell if he can become famous living his life after incarceration, maybe there's hope for me. God has a plan for all of us and as a frat brother once told me, "HE puts us where HE wants us". You can't "Unlive where you're from and if you can have "Church" on a dirt road with a congregation of one or in a 6 by 9 cell, let these "INSPIRATIONS FROM THE PHATBOY" take off and "Git Er Dun". I can see my English teachers cringing now, but

I sincerely hope you will enjoy my "Inspirations". PHATBOY Phil Marcha, March 2024

COMING FULL CIRCLE

Coming Full Circle, coming back home Learning life's lessons, uncovering stones. Running the fast lane, teetering on the ledge. I 'm coming full circle, and it gives me the edge.

When I was young, still tucked in the nest. I dreamed of the day; I could head out west. To become a man, was always the plan. My father guided me with his stiff hand.

A son of my own now, with each passing day, I try and guide him, to make his own way. Now I'm sure, this path that I'm on, It's the circle of life, that's taking me home.

Coming full circle, coming back home. Learning the lessons from uncovered stones. Throttling back to the right lane, planning my next move, I'm coming full circle, still searching for truth.

Soon I know, my time will run out, I won't have the strength to fight the next bout. But with each mile that passes me by, I head west, where mountains touch the sky.

It's up in the Hills, I know I'm at my best, Knowing that soon, I'll be laid to rest. It's been a great ride, I've been "Bad to the Bone", The last leg of this circle, that's taking me home.

I'm COMING FULL CIRCLE out here on my own. Learned many lessons; turned my last stone. I'm at the last exit of this journey I'm on, I've COME FULL CIRCLE , I'm finally home.

PHATBOY Phil Marcha August 2013

The inspiration to write this came to me on the ride to Sturgis in 2013. Although I'd been to the rally many times since my maiden trip in 2000, this hot August trip, I rode my Road King through Oklahoma, Texas, Kansas, Nebraska, and finally South Dakota. And it wasn't the most scenic. But on the flip side I had plenty of time on the bike to reflect on my life, where I'd been and where I was headed. I had just emptied my savings and opened PHATBOY PHILS STEAKHOUSE and APRIL'S HIDE OUT, which was the bar right across the street from the restaurant. The Black Hills of South Dakota were calling me for a step out of the fast lane. There is a uniqueness about the Black Hills that is filled with history above and beyond the Sturgis bike rally. Mount Rushmore, Crazy Horse, Needles, Deadwood, Lead, Custer, Hill City, the Bad Lands, Spearfish Canyon, Devil's Tower and "No Panty Wednesday", Buffalo Chip with their concerts, the Full Throttle Saloon, Gunners and One-Eyed Jacks, the Knuckle, the Iron Horse, Glencoe Campground, my oh my , I could go on forever. You must experience it one time whether it's during the rally or not. It's Biker Heaven and God painted a picture in the Black Hills of South Dakota.

LEFT HAND LOW

Wherever you go, all bikers should know, The unwritten rules of the ride. Most bikers know, it ain't for show, A simple greeting we all should abide. Other bikers we meet, with a wave we greet. Simply said just a friendly hello, Tucked in your seat, when you're on the street. It's just a gesture; it's LEFT HAND LOW.

It's the biker way, consistent every day, To show some respect, to those not yet met, From near or far, wherever you are, It's not for show it's LEFT HAND LOW.

LEFT HAND LOW, it's meant to approve, LEFT HAND LOW, we're all in the groove, LEFT HAND LOW, thumb up towards the sky LEFT HAND LOW, freedom for life.

From Sturgis and the Black Hills, The Dragon and Keys, Beartooth, Million Dollar Highway, the Blueridge, The rides are just a few of these. Highways and parkways, peaks and passes. Switchbacks and curves rode on PHAT asses. With freedom in mind, we all choose to find, This thing that we know, it's LEFT HAND LOW.

Brothers and sisters, we ride with no bias, Harley, Indian, Jap bikes, ya don't have to like us. Respect should be given, by this gesture we show, Whatever you ride, it's LEFT HAND LOW.

LEFT HAND LOW, it's meant to approve, LEFT HAND LOW, we're still in the groove, LEFT HAND LOW, look to the skies, LEFT HAND LOW, freedom for life.

So, when you're out on your ride, And HE'S right by your side, Sent down from heaven above, This gesture of respect and love, A simple greeting this I know. Heaven sent to those down below. All bikers should definitely know, This thing we call LEFT HAND LOW.

PHATBOY Phil Marcha August 2015

The inspiration for this writing was on the way to Sturgis in 2015 which was the 75th Rally. While still in Texas, my clutch cable wore a tiny hole in my oil filter, and it started leaking. By the time we got to Albuquerque New Mexico, I got it to a dealership and got a new filter and an oil change. Readjusted the clutch cable and headed to Durango. Well, by adjusting the clutch cable, the clutch had loosened so the next day I took it to another dealership, and they fixed it. Then my back tire and wheel started a "shimmy" and it progressively got worse. After riding the Tetons and Yellowstone, I could only run about 40 to 45 mph. So, I told the other six riders to go on ahead and I'd meet them in Sturgis. They were used to doing 80 to 90 mph. The rest of the way through Wyoming was slow but I had time to reflect on my 45 years of riding a bike. Our first bike, my three brothers and I, was a Kawasaki Dynamite 75 cc. Dad took us to the bank to get a loan. Our payment was $15 a month and we paid for it by doing odd jobs and the best job ever, picking up aluminum cans from bar parking lots and dumpsters on Saturday and Sunday mornings. Those were the days my friends. Gas was 29 cents a gallon and we rode that little bike from sunup till sundown taking turns. When it broke down, Dad would fix it and off we would go again. I'd come a long way from that bike, and many others that I paid for to a Road King. Just like a fellow Okie Roger Miller sang, I was "King of the Road". But I sure wish I had mechanical Dad on that ride. When I finally made it to Sturgis, I got it into an old hippie biker mechanic. He diagnosed it as "loose spokes". He tightened my spokes up, then I got married. What a trip!

RUN FOR ETERNITY

Here's your invitation, For a ride full of fun, You just might find salvation, Get on your bike and run. To the Black Hills and Sturgis, Or the Dragon in Tennessee, We'll even do Daytona, Then go ride the Keys.

Dust off your leathers, Strap on your Harley boots, Get ready to face some weather, On this run, you'll find your roots. Deadwood, Rushmore or Devil's Tower, "I'll go where you want me to go", Crazy Horse, the Bad Lands, or Custer, I'll even freeze in Jackson Hole.

Join me in this RUN FOR ETERNITY, Have faith and trust in Him, This winding road is certainly, A great journey these places I've been.

Needles, Four Corners, the Million Dollar Highway, Route 66, Spearfish Canyon, and Sparks, Run with me I'll lead the way, Let's ride before it's dark. I know "There's a train a comin'", Just like in Durango and Silverton, Best get your house in order, If you're "Riding with the Son".

I love to count my blessings, These places that I've been, So, climb aboard with me, Let the road wash away your sin.

Come make this RUN FOR ETERNITY, Have faith, and trust in the man, Believe me this ride is certainly, A chance to welcome in His Plan.

PHATBOY Phil Marcha August 2022

I wrote this on my 2022 trip to Sturgis, my first since 2015 and post Covid. That year I saw Lynard Skynyrd at the Buffalo Chip with my bro Kyle W. He's in the "SIMPLE MAN" club and he and his wife Brenda (she made the "Stairway to Heaven" trip)…RIP…broke my Sturgis cherry in 2000 when I took off from Altus and made this trip in my '71heavy half Chevy pulling a two-horse trailer that I had converted into a bike trailer for my '91 pro street shovelhead fat boy and camping gear. How red neck was that? It was late July and of course it was hot. I drove all night dodging deer from Dodge City Kansas to Valentine Nebraska. I met them the next day at the Redbud Casino just across the border in South Dakota. When we finally made it to Sturgis, my eyes opened wide as if I'd never seen these many bikes. Over one million bikers attended the Millenium rally. Are you kidding me? Normally, about 6 to 7 hundred thousand bikers attend the rally. How apropos we stayed in the Hog Heaven campground that year as I have most of the years since I've been going. Thank you, Kyle and Brenda, for introducing me to "Biker Paradise" and the Black Hills of South Dakota.

PRISON

My time with the Oklahoma Department of Corrections at the State Reformatory facility in Granite Oklahoma was certainly an eye-opener. Needing health insurance, I took a position that I felt overqualified for in food service in the chow hall of the reformatory, but I needed health insurance. Supervising 20 inmate orderlies to prepare 3 "hots" 24/7 365 for over 1000 prisoners was quite a challenge. Once my "you get what you give" philosophy was implemented, it was easy running's. I took the approach of "THERE'S NO FUTURE IN THE PAST" and when the orderlies realized I had access to their "jackets" and never once looked, well I gained some "street cred" and felt they respected me. They had already been judged and who was I to judge their past? Many "lifers" where just doing their time before they met the judge of all judges. Some of the things that I have done in my life could have landed me behind those walls. I was just lucky enough to never get caught. The first Thanksgiving dinner we prepared and served, I sat in the middle of the chow hall and distributed orange cups and sporks. These men, many older than me, were so grateful and some mentioned it was the best meal they'd ever had since their incarceration (some well over 60 years). Now talk about the true meaning of Thanksgiving. That day was a message and a blessing from the MAN UPSTAIRS and it forever changed my perspective on food service.

INSIDE LOOKING OUT
OUTSIDE LOOKING IN

INSIDE LOOKING OUT, OUTSIDE LOOKING IN "Just doin my time", repayment for my sin. Walls of stone, and bars of steel, Can't erase, the way I feel. Eyes on eyes seems to be the way, Lord help see me, through another day. Another count, will eventually clear, I'm finally accepting what landed me here.

OUTSIDE LOOKING IN, INSIDE LOOKING OUT I know the reason, there is no doubt. To be a better man, It's part of HIS plan. And it ain't that hard, This life on the yard, If you play by the rules, And you don't act like a fool.

INSIDE LOOKING OUT, OUTSIDE LOOKING IN I'm just doin' the best I can, You get what you give, when it comes to respect Some of these men, haven't learned that yet. I remain committed, and take the honest stand, With God's direction, to love my fellow man. Paying for your sins has got to be the way. Surely, we'll find grace, on our final judgement day.

PHATBOY Phil Marcha October 2021

The inspiration for this started churning in my head the first couple of weeks of working at the reformatory. The old Grand Funk Railroad song "Inside Looking Out" kept on and on playing in my head. Although I had heard this song dozens of times since the early 70's, I felt like I was "Closer to Home" to what Mark Farner sang about in this song. Even though I didn't have to live 100% behind these walls, I felt I had a better understanding of the life they were living. Now of course, I had the luxury to go home every night, but I was beginning to understand what these men felt on the daily. Now some phycologists would diagnose the "Stockholm Syndrome", but I'd rather use the analogy of "walk a mile in my shoes" or "don't judge a book by its cover". Both seemed apropos in this situation, and I was glad to be learning this life lesson.

GYM ON THE YARD

I wake up early in the morning, Getting up is sometimes hard. But these men are expecting, GYM ON THE YARD.

The "make it take it "pickup games, Running up and down the floor, The anticipation in their eyes, Waiting for me to unlock the door.

The dust from the volleyball pit, Jammin' in the band room, Grab a guitar and have a sit, And strum away your blues.

Horseshoes or handball, A few rounds with the heavy bag, Foosball, ping pong, or just chop it up, Come to the Wilson Gym, you will be glad.

At the end of the day, The fellowship we shared, It's meant to show in the way, For our fellow man we cared.

Music, push-ups, or shoot a game of pool, Throw some bones or Magic cards, If you don't act a fool, all is cool. Come get some Rec, at the GYM ON THE YARD!

PHATBOY "Coach" Phil Marcha July 2022

During this time, I saw my role transition from food service in the chow hall, to being the recreation officer or "Coach" of the prison. An inmate that was responsible for the prison newspaper asked me if I had anything that I wanted to publish. I sat down and wrote this in about ten minutes. My "time" in this position was even more gratifying than in the chow hall. So many of the prisoners appreciated me and my orderlies for what we provided in the way of recreation. I definitely had a tight crew, and we rocked GYM ON THE YARD!!

CERTIFICATE OF APPRECIATION
OKLAHOMA STATE REFORMATORY
INMATE COUNCIL

This Certificate is awarded to

COACH PHIL

ificate is awarded to you in appreciation for the service and work tha
in making the 'First Annual Fun Day' a successful event. The effort
the Inmate Council can only be accomplished by the service perform
ing to sacrifice the time and efforts it takes to mo... 's A a succe
lity. We thank you for your service and commitment... the Inmate

AT THE END OF THE DAY

Up in the morning, at 7 o'clock, My dedication to my work, will never stop. This prison gym, where they come to play, Just trying to make a difference, by THE END OF THE DAY.

I try my best to give and get respect, To these men here trying to pay their debt. It's difficult at times, I try to find a way, To give direction , AT THE END OF THE DAY.

I don't question the reasons why they are here, Sending a message, only GOD should they fear. "Life is hard on the yard", I heard an inmate say. The challenge is just making it, till THE END OF THE DAY.

Doing time, sure ain't easy, I see it in their eyes. And every minute, they're just trying to survive. All I can do, is by example show the right way, I'm just a "Simple Man", AT THE END OF THE DAY.

It's hard to balance the rights and the wrongs. They find "Pride and Joy", playing their favorite songs. The little things in life, finding the words to say, I hope I've made a difference, by THE END OF THEIR STAY!!

PHATBOY Phil Marcha August 2023

On this day, the prison was on lockdown. This time, the reason that was given was there an incident at another state yard between the "Crips" and the "Bloods", In corrections the SOP was when there is gang on gang conflicts, every DOC facility goes on lock down. This meant they were confined to their units and depending on the severity of the incident, possible confinement to their cells. Recreation at the gym is normally suspended during lockdown. This meant none of my orderlies would be coming to the gym to perform their duties and I had to sit in the gym, all day long, with nothing much to do but my administrative duties. Now OSR was supposed to be an "Honor Yard" with no active gang members. This is when I learned the meaning of "Blood In, Blood Out". During this lock down, which lasted a couple weeks, administration decided to "reassign" cells for the "Bloods". All the 30 supposed "Bloods" came to the gym with their gear and belongings to be held there while the COs (correctional officers) figured out their new cell assignments. I noticed that my lead band orderly was sitting by himself very close to the band room which was right by my office. When I got the chance, I went to talk to him. I was very surprised when he said, "I guess I woke up a Blood" today. I asked him to further explain. He told me that when he was in his youth, he was affiliated with the "Crips" but was no longer active. This was potentially a very bad situation, but he had the respect of the other "Bloods" as they knew him and knew he was not active. I don't know who was more scared, me or him. Thank God for "YARD HONOR".

25

YARD HONOR

Sitting behind these walls of stone I'm forced to accept a lot of things. Unwritten rules, agreed upon by these men, It's only what YARD HONOR brings. Yes, the "police" will have their way, Constant counts and locking gates, The mundane daily and hourly routines, Will ultimately affect their fate. It's kind of noble in its own way, These "gentlemen agreements " they have, And live by every day.

It's called "YARD HONOR".

Nothing written on paper, And you don't have to buy in. Only God's grace will save you, When you're paying for your sins.

And snitches get stitches, Heed the word of the "shot caller", You don't want to be labeled a Bitch, Not everyone can be the "Baller". It's just like prison tats, They all have their special meaning. And if you don't read them right, Your ignorance could leave you bleeding.

Believe in YARD HONOR.

Now I'm not about to say, That these things are always right, But if you don't respect the "word", You may damn sure end up in a fight. You may think it's absurd and not real, Behind the stone, bars and razor wire, Men living in 6 by 9's your front door is steel. It's not a life you should desire.

Just go along to get along, And respect those that came before. Accept these rules you won't be wrong, You'll make it through the day, "FO SHO".

Respect some YARD HONOR

The inspiration for this, in my opinion, was the way the prisoners interacted with each other daily. Men from all races, different places, different raising and different countries, are forced to "get along" with each other. There are no left or right agendas. There's no constitution or bill of rights on the yard. They, for the most part, "police" themselves. Now when things get real, the COs and administration step in, but that is rare. It's normally the "prison" way or YARD HONOR. And it's too bad that we, on the outside, can't live with HONOR anymore. Back in the day, you shook a man's hand, looked him in the eyes, and kept your word. Once you've been behind the "walls", there's nowhere to run and you better respect YARD HONOR. Trust me, "You get what you give, and give what you get".

HONOR'S GONE

Back in the day, your word was your bond. I ask the question, where has HONOR GONE? You looked in the eyes, you shook a hand. No one questioned, what is your plan? No need for contracts or things written down. Commitment was solid; words were sound . Where has it GONE. This thing called HONOR. Trust in spoken words, is no longer.

HONOR'S GONE; how do we get it back? Character and honesty are often attacked. We owe it to our kids and kids kids. To teach them HONOR, leave nothing hid. The deception and straight up lies. Even when people look you in the eyes. Call me "Old School" I ain't no fool. My HONOR, I guarantee is spot on true.

HONOR was taught by my father. And he HONORED my mother. They spent many years together. They survived some stormy weather. It wasn't easy growing up. But what we had was just enough. A debt to my son, I pray, and I pass it on. I'm sad to say, HONORS GONE.

PHATBOY Phil Marcha August 2024

The inspiration for this simply put is the deterioration of family values. I'm not going to debate the reasons why as there are many. I'm simply going to say that we, as parents and grandparents, owe it to our predecessors to do a much better job teaching our youth these "Tuff Love" lessons. Take a few minutes every day to sit and talk with these youngsters and give them "Old School" advice and analogies for their consumption. Let them ask questions. Pass on to them what we were taught. Then do a lot of praying that somehow, some way, it sinks in.

PRAY IT UP

Behind these walls, I see a lot of things, Acts of kindness, that the good Lord brings. Instilled in these men, I sometimes find, Talks with HIM, and efforts to be kind. Heads bowed, grace before sup, They ask for blessings; they PRAY IT UP.

PRAY IT UP, PRAY IT UP, We learned it early, when we were just pups. When you ask of HIM, he will fill your cup, And when you're in doubt, PRAY IT UP.

Unanswered prayers, sometimes the norm, But talks with HIM, help weather the storm. Hand to hand, and man to man, There is no doubt, it's part of his plan. No need to argue, no need to buck, I'm asking you my brothers to PRAY IT UP.

PRAY IT UP, PRAY IT UP, Learning life's lessons, while growing up. When you ask of HIM, he will fill your cup, If you take the time to, PRAY IT UP.

The days pass by, as I grow older, I ask myself why the nights seem a bit colder. It's talks with HIM, that get me through. I ask for forgiveness, to start anew. Prayers for strength, on the wall I'm backed up. I find blessings when I PRAY IT UP.

PRAY IT UP, PRAY IT UP, Learning life lessons, we're no longer pups When you ask of HIM, he will fill your cup, Stay in faith my friends, and STAY PRAYED UP.

PHATBOY Phil Marcha May 2021

The inspiration for PRAY IT UP came from one of my Hispanic orderlies. Now for the most part, in the chow hall, there were no seconds, no extras, and "no mas". But the orderlies, once the entire yard was served, could fill their trays with all the leftover food they wanted. Well, this particular kitchen orderly worked as a line server, meaning he worked on "the line". The "line" was a long steam table where pans of food set down in "steam wells" to keep hot food hot and cold food cold (ice replaced steam). Each pan of food had one orderly assigned to portion out the food onto multi-compartment trays. When trays had the proper amount of food in them, they were then distributed to each inmate. This particular orderly, who I considered "me amigo", would load up his tray, then go out in the chow hall and distribute "seconds" to other inmates. Now this "extra" food he could have eaten or put in a "clam shell" (Togo box) to take back to his cell. Now neither of these things, giving extras to inmates or taking food back to your cell, were allowed by policy. But how can you deny acts of kindness and unselfishness like this? And if you've ever been in a county jail, the food we threw away every day could get you many favors and even money put on your "books". When he was done distributing the extra food to other inmates, he would ask if there was anything else I needed him to do, and head back to his cell. But the last thing he would say to me every day was, "hey boss, STAY PRAYED UP". At Christmas that year, I made about a dozen wooden crosses. I snuck them through the x-ray machine as they could have been considered "contraband" and gave them to some of my orderlies. I gave him one and told him "STAY PRAYED UP".

CHURCH

I grew up in the Methodist church. At Grace United Methodist Church, my first Sunday school teacher was Ol' Miss Margaret, a classy but stern wife of a cotton farmer. This is an iconic lady from SW Oklahoma. She and my mother, who was the youth choir director, were very close friends. I lost my mother to Covid in 2021 and Ol' Miss Margaret stepped right in to lend her support in that role. When I put in my first restaurant, Main Street Grill, I was right across the street from First United Methodist church where me and my first wife were married in the summer of 1983. The pastor of the church, at that time, ask if I would direct the "Wow Wednesday" meal and I happily accepted. At the time, the meal was in the fellowship hall that was underneath the sanctuary in the basement. At that time, I fed 50 to 60 people, but the plan was to build a family life center with classrooms, a basketball court and a 6-figure commercial kitchen. What an opportunity. Once the facility was completed, my meals soon grew to 200 to 250. The Consecration Dedication of the family life center meant a meal for the over 600 members of the church. With the help of a great crew of "elders", and God's inspiration, we made it happen. A classmate of mine who was a district judge mentioned to me that I was doing a "great ministry". I was truly taken back and thought of myself, a minister? Hardly! But the more I thought about what he had said, the more motivated I was to live up to the title of minister of food. I guess I conceded that I did have a God given talent and when some of the women would come up to me and thank me for letting them take a night off from cooking for their families…. I finally understood my little part in the "ministry" of the church and felt blessed with gratification.

OL' MISS MARGARET

She was a cotton farmer's wife, Lived in Oklahoma, all her life. She was a mother of two fine men, I'm honored to call them my friends.

OL'MISS MARGARET

She was out of the "old School" mold, May I honor her, may I be so bold? At Grace, she was my Sunday school teacher. Truth be known; she could have been the preacher.

OL' MISS MARGARET

She was a strong woman, full of class, Raised to be a lady, from a small lass. She was iconic in every way. Proud to have known her, I must say.

OL' MISS MARGARET

She had so much dedication for our community. She was so generous, with her philanthropy. She hosted many parties; man, they were fun. I'm going to miss her when she's gone.

OL' MISS MARGARET

Young ladies, you should try and be, More like OL" MISS MARGARET for your family. She was one in a million, I can surely attest. One of God's angels on earth, she was the best.

OL' MISS MARGARET

PHATBOY Phil Marcha July 4th, 2023

Obviously, the inspiration for writing this came early in my life and has continued until today. Margaret Worrell has been a part of my life for over a half century. She is one of the classiest ladies I've ever met. Her endeavors with MAIN STREET ALTUS have won awards on the state level. Every October, the Worrells hosted a "Halloween" party. Many years she would ask me to cook some of my "Cotton Picking" award winning chili. The family were great customers of mine. Maragret loved the mash potato cakes I learned from my grandma Selvey and of course the men loved my steaks. Her family has been an integral part of the cotton community in SW Oklahoma, but beyond those accomplishments, she is an Icon, short and sweet!! OL' MISS MARGARET.

WHAT GOD DIDN'T DO

I've come to know, when it comes to praying, If you listen, you'll hear what he's saying. Sometimes prayers don't go your way. Just be patient, there will be another day. So have faith and just be cool, It's not what He did, it's what He didn't do.

WHAT GOD DIDN'T DO, often hard to swallow. WHAT GOD DIDN'T DO, trust me, just follow. WHAT GOD DIDN'T DO, accept what He did. WHAT GOD DIDN'T DO; there's nothing He hid.

The struggles of life often are hard. The end of your journey will seem very far. Even when angry, the prayers that you pray, Left unanswered at the end of the day. It's still just a journey, this ride that we're on. Some truth lies here, in the lyrics of my song. Written with faith, what I've been called to do, It's not what He did, it's what He didn't do.

WHAT GOD DIDN'T DO, often hard to swallow. WHAT GOD DIDN'T DO, still you must follow. WHAT GOD DIDN'T DO, accept what He does WHAT GOD DIDN'T DO, is shown by His love.

Don't get discouraged or ask the reasons why. He knows your path; there's no reason to cry. It's hard not knowing, understanding your asks. It's in His message; it's in HIS task. Trust His motives and have faith in Him. Wondering why He didn't answer, it not a sin. Accept what He does, understand His tool. It's not what He did, it's what He didn't do.

WHAT GOD DIDN'T DO, often hard to swallow. WHAT GOD DIDN'T DO, have faith to follow. WHAT GOD DIDN'T DO, believe what I say. WHAT GOD DIDN'T DO; He will lead the way.

The inspiration for this writing came from hearing my Pastor Paul give his testimony during a sermon. After graduating from OU's pharmacy school, he was trying to gain employment. He prayed and prayed and prayed for a job in the pharmacy industry. His prayers remained unanswered. He became angry after dedicating many years to his chosen profession. So, he prayed once again and asked for God's direction and strength. God answered his prayer by leading him to Oral Roberts Seminary school then his ordainment in the Methodist Church. Paul finally opened his own church in West Moore, Oklahoma, and that venture has been very successful. I 100% believe that God has a plan for all of us, and He puts us where He wants us at times in our life. It's up to us to trust Him and have faith that HIS HAND, will lead us!!!

LORD LIFT UP YOUR HAND

WHAT'S GOING ON in the world is CRAZY. I CAN'T TELL YOU WHY people are so lazy. But with each passing day, When I hit my knees to pray. Marvin Gaye said it best, WHAT'S GOING ON is TRULY the test. Hag sang, ARE THE GOOD TIMES REALLY OVER? But I'm still looking for CLOSURE. MY SWEET LORD, can you LIFT UP YOUR HAND? And SHOW ME THE WAY to be a BETTER MAN.

Is it time to COME TOGETHER? And avoid the STORMY WEATHER. The things we see in the press, Proves to me the country is in a mess. What we see on social media and TV, From Boys to Men, ON BENDED KNEE. To Sam Cook's, WHAT A WONDERFUL WORLD THIS COULD BE. The Doobie Brothers sang TAKEN IT TO THE STREETS. Will ALL THE LONELY PEOPLE make it complete? Is it time MY SWEET LORD, to LIFT UP YOUR HAND? Questions of RIGHT OR WRONG, for this SIMPLE MAN. Will HE answer with THE THUNDER ROLLS? Or will He SAVE ME, and SAVE MY SOUL?

The thing that worries me the most, For my family, are the unseen ghosts. The SMILIN FACES that hide behind agendas, And BACK STABBERS that should offend ya. But LOVES IN NEED OF LOVE TODAY. And there's got to be a BETTER WAY. Before we become DUST IN THE WIND, You need to know YOU'VE GOT A FRIEND.

Is it time MY SWEET LORD, to LIFT UP YOUR HAND? And COME TOGETHER and SAVE THE LAND.

For LIFE'S HIWAY, is a JOURNEY we're on. SONGS IN THE KEY OF LIFE, can't be wrong.

PHATBOY Phil Marcha May 2022

We were on "lock down" which meant no one was coming to the prison and I was ALL BY MYSELF, KILLIN TIME in my office, on my computer, surfing You-Tube. I decided to have a bit of fun and write this while listening to the songs I was surfing. Many of these songs were by artists from the 60's and 70's and I HAD EM ON 8-TRACK. Later in this book you will see another "fun" poem titled HAD EM ON 8-TRACK, again about the music I had on 8-track. I'm in the middle of writing a book titled the same. But we'll save those things for later.

HIS HAND

Times are getting harder, all the time. Some questions, I write down in this rhyme. Have we passed the point of no return? Or are we on the path of eternal burn? Do we make the effort to "Just Get Along"? Is our faith, in HIS HAND, truly that strong? Do acts of kindness enter your mind? Answers to these questions, I'm trying to find.

Where is HIS HAND, in times of need? Where is HIS HAND, to stop the bleed? Does HIS HAND comfort those in grief? Does HIS HAND pick up those that believe?

The path that we're on seems filled with doubt. I see the lost, looking for ways out. It's troubling times here in the fold. The days are hot, the nights seem cold. As I sit and wonder, all day long. Is HIS HAND truly that strong? To lift us up out of this mess. Those that have faith, will they be blessed?

Where is HIS HAND, in times of need? Where is HIS HAND, to stop the bleed? Where is HIS HAND, in times like this? Where is HIS HAND, is there something I've missed?

Does HIS HAND comfort those who have lost? Does HIS HAND give to those in need the most? Will HIS HAND give direction towards our goals? Is time running out for salvation of our souls?

Let's trust that HIS HAND will lead the way. And tomorrow will be a better day. With the little time we all have left, You must have faith we will be blessed. Just make an attempt to do what's right, When you get down on your knees at night. Ask for forgiveness, for here's what's at stake, A chance to look in His eyes, and HIS HAND to shake.

PHATBOY Phil Marcha December 2022

It's now been over two years since I put "pen to paper" to write HIS HAND. Things really haven't improved much, in fact as of a couple of months ago, I feel like things have gotten worse. I'll keep sending up prayers and hope they will get answered. I try to stay strong in my faith that someday we can all live in peace. I have a challenge for you. Every day search out someone who you don't know and try to pass on a little kindness. Whether it's opening a door for seniors or helping little old ladies with their groceries at Wal-Mart or paying for a Vet's meal or turning off the TV and spending time with your grandchildren or spending an hour or two at your church helping with whatever. Find a way to lend a HAND with someone who "Needs a Favor" and maybe, just maybe, HIS HAND will touch you in your time of need.

BETTER MAN

Looking back, reliving my past, Not too proud of some of the things I've done. Times were crazy, my life was so fast. Too much ignorance, too much fun. Much too often, I didn't have a care, To those precious few I hurt. Going through life, totally unaware. Some of my actions were absolutely the worst.

Time is quickly, passing me by. "Coming Full Circle" is the test. To become a BETTER MAN, I promise I'll try. And through my actions, I'll give it my best. It's hard, you see, to live with regrets. Water has run under the bridge. Opportunities each day surely presents. Redemption forthcoming, with this I pledge.

Looking for forgiveness, and having faith, Through the hourglass runs sand. My commitment so I sayeth, To try to be a BETTER MAN. I wake up every day with good intentions. And try not to wear a mask. These things that haunt me, I won't mention. I know, "There's No Future In The Past".

To be a BETTER MAN, is truly my goal. And that's my current path. Lord, please help me save my soul. And save me from your wrath. I pray for forgiveness, and I'll have faith. And each day, recommit to my plan. I pray God puts on my plate. The strength I need to become a BETTER MAN.

PHATBOY Phil Marcha January 2023

The inspiration for this? A lifetime of f-ing up, plain and simple. The Eagles wrote the lyrics, "Life in the fast lane, surely make you lose your mind". I can certainly agree. Attending college, and when I was in my 20's, some of the things I did could have, should have, landed me "behind bars". Thank God it did. After college I went to work for Spur's and Graham

Central Station, two of the biggest "bars" in Oklahoma. How Ironic?? And thank God for this thing called "FORGIVENESS", "God is great, beer is good, and people are crazy"!!

FORGIVENESS

On life's highway, people do you wrong. And some vendettas last way too long. No one is exempt from their sins. Places we went and should not have been. We've eaten fruit from forbidden trees. And we've been knocked down to our knees. But here's the thing, it's just a test. We should be searching for FORGIVENESS.

It's been said we should forgive and forget. I must admit, I've not mastered that yet. You see it's hard, when you've been dissed. This lesson of love, somehow, I missed. But I'm starting to mellow, it's never too late. This circle of life will decide my fate. If I accept this life lesson, I hope I'll be blessed. Still looking for this thing called FORGIVENESS.

To be forgiven, you must forgive. It's been a few years that I have lived. And "Sorry seems to be the hardest word". Living in denial, I've learned, is absurd. He knows what's been done, & knows your past The end of the day, can't hide behind your mask. For He is merciful, someday I'll be blessed. It's all in His hand, He'll grant FORGIVENESS.

PHATBOY Phil Marcha February 2023

Probably one of the hardest lessons I've ever had to learn and am still learning is FORGIVENESS. As I've said before, as many times that I've messed up in my life, and the people I hurt by either my words or my actions, I'm glad there's FORGIVENESS. It's hard sometimes to forgive those that have hurt me or my family. There are many bible verses that address FORGIVENESS. And if you will allow me, my favorite is Luke 6:37. "Forgive and you will be forgiven". It doesn't get no plainer than that! Can I get an amen?

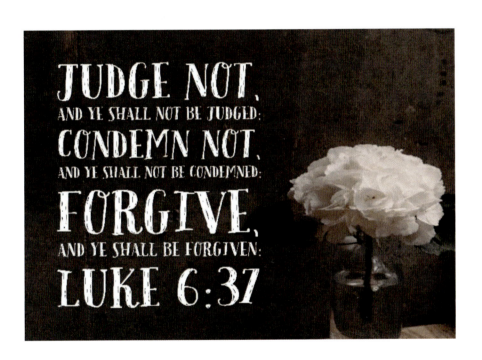

WALK WITH ME

As we go down this road called "Life". We may stumble, and we may fall. Be certain that sometimes it's a fight. But WALK WITH ME, and we'll stand tall.

"Don't Walk in front, I may not follow", " Don't walk behind me, as I may not lead". Just WALK WITH ME, not waiting for tomorrow. Side by side, hand in hand, is what we need.

There are barriers and blocks in the road. And obstacles that get in the way. WALK WITH ME, I'll carry the load. Together we'll make our way.

I don't know where we're heading, But I'm certain on where we've been. Mistakes of our past, we should be shedding. WALK WITH ME and have thick skin.

The journey we're on is long and winding. Sometimes we carry a heavy load. Our brotherhood is for sure binding. WALK WITH ME, till the fork in the road.

Not sure who will go first. And pass on to the great beyond. I know with love my heart will burst. You WALKED WITH ME; there's no denying our bond.

PHATBOY Phil Marcha February 2023

The inspiration for this poem came in the winter of 2023. We were on "lock-down" at the prison and as I told you before, I was by myself in the quiet gym. Now me being an Alpha, this was a very hard lesson to learn for me. Realize that I'm not normally one to follow, probably never will be. And if you followed me down every "wrong" path that I've been down, good chance you'd be "locked up" or worse. I've truly been blessed by never getting caught with some of the deeds I've done. Working at the prison gave me some reflection on my past. It also gave me some inspiration to be a BETTER MAN. There is a term in prison "Dead man walking" and if you saw the Green Mile, you understand. Merle Haggard's song "Sing Me Back Home" identifies my analogy. And its definitely motivation to never WALK THAT WALK.

SHINE THE LIGHT

In these troubled days filled with darkness, It's a must to remain focused. Stay strong keep fighting the fight, Have faith and SHINE THE LIGHT.

When one goes down on accident, Don't give up and become complacent. Pick up the torch and know you're right, And continue to SHINE THE LIGHT.

The question of where we are heading, As our faith continues growing. Let's keep our goal in sight, With eyes wide open, SHINE THE LIGHT.

Even if your mentor is broken, And his words remain unspoken. Side by side with prayer we fight, In his honor, SHINE THE LIGHT.

So, join me my faithful brothers, Even if we come from different mothers. Become a disciple of what is right, Pick up the torch to SHINE THE LIGHT.

His work in faith not finished, The situation may be a blemish. To the end of the earth I'll fight, For my Pastor Paul, I'LL SHINE THE LIGHT.

PHATBOY Phil Marcha MAY 2023

The inspiration for this came about a year before I wrote this. My Pastor Paul (who I've mentioned before), had his second stroke in ten years. The first one he had wasn't too bad as he was still able to communicate, walk, play golf and numerous other functions of normal life. After a brief recovery, he was even able to perform his life's passion in preaching and running his church at West Moore Community Church in Moore Oklahoma. Now Paul is my pledge brother, fraternity brother, was in my first wedding and like I mentioned before, performed my second wedding via the phone when my wife and I were married in Sturgis in 2015. Through the years he has helped me with my faith. He convinced me to "let go of the reins" sometimes and let the "man" upstairs be the driver. Now me being and alpha, I've struggled with this at times in my life. To say I'm "controlling" would be a very true understatement. His second stroke was far worse. He had to retire from his position of senior pastor at the church he built. Although his speech is limited and he's bound to a wheelchair, he's still fighting the fight. I still stop by for visits and ball games and bring him an occasional chocolate milk shake. I wrote SHINE THE LIGHT to honor Paul and his work and to challenge OUr fraternity brothers to do what they can to carry Pastor Paul's "Light". Even though he's not the man he used to be, as many of us are not, I thank God that "I'M NOT THE MAN I USED TO BE" …trust me, it's a good thing. And I thank Pastor Paul for being a part of my life in showing me "THE LIGHT".

NOT THE MAN I USED TO BE

Sand through the hourglass, moves so slow, "Life in the fast lane", I was living out of control. Now I find myself, more time on bended knees. And realizing, I'm NOT THE MAN I USED TO BE.

It's hard to accept, this "getting old" thing. It's hard not knowing what tomorrow will bring. I used to be bullet proof and could chop down trees. Hard to admit, I'm NOT THE MAN I USED TO BE.

The circle of life is beginning to close in. Hope the Man upstairs, let's me redeem my sin. Time is so precious; I'm beginning to see. Where did it go, I'm NOT THE MAN I USED TO BE.

It's starting to narrow, this path that I'm on. I hope one day; my words are the lyrics in a song. Time is running out; on this we can agree Accepting, I'm NOT THE MAN I USED TO BE.

It's not a bad thing, this "growing older." My family's weight rests on my shoulders. I've finally accepted, things aren't all about me. Proud to admit, I'm NOT THE MAN I USED TO BE.

PHATBOY Phil Marcha 2022

NOT THE MAN I USED TO BE (pt 2)

I'm NOT THE MAN I USED TO BE. Something happened deep inside of me. Arthritis in my hands, I've replaced my knee. I'm having challenges, trying to see.

What lies ahead? Hell, I don't know. "Life in the fast lane", has taken its toll. Had a brain tumor, but now I'm cancer free. Realizing, I'm NOT THE MAN I USED TO BE.

It's not so much, the aches and pain. But what's going on, driving me insane. I'm having moments, that scare me to death. So much to accomplish before I draw my last breath.

Worried that I haven't lived up to the legacy, Of my father, his father, & on up the family tree. It's a daily challenge, I hope you can see. I'm certainly, NOT THE MAN I USED TO BE.

I retired from working, with still work to do. Improvements are needed, in my attitude. I'm trying to write down things in my life, Trying to be a BETTER MAN, to my family, friends and wife.

I know my time will soon run out. I'll meet my maker; I have no doubt. I pray He will forgive me and hope He will see. That I'm truly NOT THE MAN I USED TO BE.

PHATBOY Phil Marcha November 2024

A sequel to the sequel. The inspiration to NOT THE MAN I USED TO BE part two, in part, Is my health deterioration. Like I said in the preface, turning 60 has been a bitch. My physical health has not had a lot of positive effects on it. When the doc's cut out my brain tumor and I did some radiation, something forever changed me. Not sure if they (the surgeons) cut out some of the "meanness", but I'm truly trying to be "kinder and gentler". Now some of my frat brothers and friends have noticed the change and sometimes comment on where's the old Phil. In a way the "Old Phil" being gone is a good thing. But being almost 65 and can't do what I used to and constant thoughts on what I can accomplish before the "Circle" is complete, well, to be honest, at times, causes stress and anxiety. And sometimes I question…. WHO'S THIS OLD MAN?

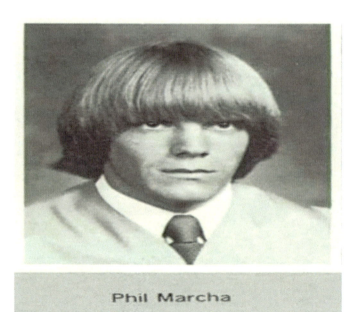

Phil Marcha

WHO'S THIS OLD MAN

WHO'S THIS OLD MAN, staring at me in the mirror? How I've changed, couldn't be any clearer. Where did time go, Hell it's been just a minute. I'm not gonna lie, I'm not gonna spin it.

I wouldn't say that I've aged well. My body is spent, I put it through Hell. It's been a great run; it's been a true test. WHO'S THIS OLD MAN, that gave his best?

WHO'S THIS OLD MAN, what have I become? Where are the days filled with fun? Seems like it happened overnight. The simplest things have become a fight.

WHO'S THIS OLD MAN, where am I going? I can hardly stand, the "not knowing". I guess I just sit back and have faith in His plan. Accept His answer to WHO'S THIS OLD MAN.

WHO'S THIS OLD MAN, yes, I've let him in. I've certainly had my share of sin. Forgiveness and mercy are my daily ask. For I'm not too proud of some of my past.

I've led a life most men only dream of. I'll just trust in the man from up above. Have faith in Him to grant me some grace. WHO'S THIS OLD MAN, my past I can't erase.

PHATBOY Phil Marcha Christmas 2024

My father is slowly getting his house in order. With retiring from work, it makes me think that I probably need to get a start on my own house. The idle time on my hands often makes me think of "Immortality" and have I done enough good or have I done too much bad? Water has run under the bridge and "THERE'S NO FUTURE IN THE PAST" but there's always tomorrow…or is there?

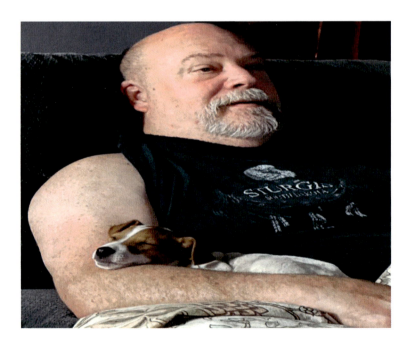

NO FUTURE IN THE PAST

Yesterday is certainly dead and gone. What lies ahead won't last for long. You can bet the sun will come up tomorrow. So be of good cheer and forget your sorrows. Let's focus on having better days. And quit living life in a cloud of haze. Stop trying to hide behind your mask. And recognize there's NO FUTURE IN THE PAST.

Under the bridge water has passed. And sand has run through the hourglass. You can't turn back the hands of time. And bridges you burned; well, you can't rewind. With each new day opportunities will arise. Have hope and faith and look to the skies. The clouds seem to be moving so fast. Realize there's NO FUTURE IN THE PAST.

There's no telling what the future holds. New stories and memories will start to unfold. The circle of life keeps closing in. Each day is a blessing, He forgives your sin. Your legacy will become your mark. Even if past deeds were sometimes dark. Put them behind you and at long last. You will find there's NO FUTURE IN THE PAST.

Broken vows, promises we failed to keep. Unanswered prayers made us lose sleep. Things are behind us so stop looking back. He grants forgiveness and that's a fact. With each new day, chances are given. Blessings are given, to change how we're livin. Have faith in Him, take off your mask. Just accept there's NO FUTURE IN THE PAST.

PHATBOY Phil Marcha March 2023

The inspiration for this comes from an old Vince Gill song of the same title. Vince is from Oklahoma and possibly one of the best true tenors in country music, Hell all of music, with no disrespect to the "Three Tenors", Bocelli or anyone else. We have all made mistakes in the past and we have all sinned. I 100% believe that there are no time machines to take you back before you did what you did or said what you said. You can't undo what's been done so get over it, learn by it, and don't do it again. Grand Funk Railroad, my first favorite band, did a song called "Stop Looking Back". Although it was never a hit, I used it many times to point out to the men in Prison that yesterday is gone. I've used it on friends even when our memories come into play. I use it with my wife, April. She became a widow in 2002 when her husband at the time, Ken, was murdered in his pawn shop as a result of a mistake made by the State of Oklahoma DOC at Granite (yes, the facility that I worked at). They released a prisoner by mistake, and he came to my hometown where Ken had his pawn shop. He held Ken at a gun point and made Ken open the safe and then pulled the trigger. At the time they had a little boy, we'll call him G. Well G never knew his father. I did, and he was a damn good man. As a young single parent due to this tragedy, April did the best she could. To this day it still haunts her. As it should. And I tell her from time to time, in our relationship, that there's NO FUTURE IN THE PAST. We all have things that we relive from our past. We all have regrets about some of our actions, with what we've said, mistakes made. Bottom line, there's not a damn thing we can do about the past but learn from it. But you can control the future for the most part. As Captain W.F. Call said in the epic series "Lonesome Dove" … .."the best thing you can do with death, is ride off from it"…I know how cold and callus that sounds. But "it is what is" and there's NO FUTURE IN THE PAST. Can I get an AMEN????

BIGGER THAN ME

I remember the message in my pastor's sermon. A light bulb went off and one thing is for certain. As "Big and Bad" as I claim to be. I'm starting to realize, life's BIGGER THAN ME.

We all had moments we didn't look beyond. We become self-centered unwilling to respond. Trust me my brothers, and on bended knee. His hand I'll shake, for He's BIGGER THAN ME.

In life we should strive to be in control. Things that we stress on will take its toll. It's hard for us alphas, we long to be free. Know that there's someone BIGGER THAN ME.

Never look back on this journey we're on. The decisions we made that turned out wrong. Stay strong in your faith, He will hear your plea. It's the "Circle of Life" and it's BIGGER THAN ME.

In closing, it took me years to admit. For it's not in my nature, & I need to submit, Mom taught me early, with a song called HE. "Proof in the puddin" HE is BIGGER THAN ME.

PHATBOY Phil Marcha December 2022

Like I mentioned before, Pastor Paul really helped me with my controlling ways and my faith. The older I get, and when life slows down, as it has, I find myself "giving in" and letting HIM take the reins more and more. Paul taught me "leap of faith" and I can't thank him enough. I have faith there is someone "BIGGER THAN ME". In the lyrics of an old Steve Wariner song : "Everything is gonna be alright, He will get you through the darkest night, when you're in HIS arms, everything will be alright". Now I'm paraphrasing just a tad, but there's no denying, and sometimes it's hard to admit, but as big as an ol' Phatboy that I is, HE"s BIGGER THAN ME!!!

FATHER TO FATHER TO FATHER

I've finally come full circle. It's taken a day or two. We've built a loving family. I'm trying to fill bigger shoes.

From great men that came before, Promises yet to keep. Shouldering my family's legacy. I got my work cut out before I sleep.

FATHER TO FATHER TO FATHER , To them I owe a debt. FATHER TO FATHER TO FATHER, My right to the name, I haven't earned yet.

The bloodlines that run deep, Flowing in the veins of thoroughbreds. Verified by your daily actions, And not the words you said.

This thing we know as honor. It is earned and not given for free. It comes from respect and hard work, I'm trying to honor our family tree.

FATHER TO FATHER TO FATHER, Framework to become a man.

FATHER TO FATHER TO FATHER, Is taught by loving and stiff hands.

We came from boys to men, It's the path that we are on. Mistakes are often made, When deciding right from wrong.

But if you pray for strength, And guidance from the Man. FATHER TO FATHER TO FATHER, Is groundwork for His plan.

FATHER TO FATHER TO FATHER, Brothers you have to trust. FATHER TO FATHER TO FATHER, Trust in God the FATHER, is truly a must.

PHATBOY Phil Marcha July 2023

The inspiration for this once again came from my FATHER. His dedication to family and church went hand in hand. When we moved from New Jersey to Oklahoma in the summer of '69, mom and dad joined Grace United Methodist Church. Dad immediately became involved with Methodist Men and was the troop leader of the Boy Scout and Cub Scout programs as there were four boys in our family. We were all very active in boy scouts. Dad figured it was a way to keep us out of trouble and out of Mom's hair. Those days were filled with many fond memories, especially camping and the Pine Wood Derby. We kind of had an advantage as dad's mechanical knowledge gave us an edge in every race. My childhood friend Andy, still to this day, bitches about this as his dad was a lawyer. His dad and my dad are still the best of friends and still sit on the board of the church. Dad later built the new sanctuary addition to the old church and still provides maintenance for the church when called on. At 87 he still outworks me. He's an amazing FATHER, MY POPS!!

MY POPS

To his face I called him Dad, To my friends, I called him my father. I won't mention when he made me mad, He was a damn good man to my mother. When I was in trouble it was Sir, To some he was "my old man". When I needed motivation, I'd get a spur. I don't know if he knows, I'm his biggest fan.

They say "apples don't fall far from the tree" And from seeds you grow crops. These days I find myself trying to be, More like my father, my dad, MY POPS.

It's hard to live up to the standard, The bar he set is high. The thousands of questions he had to answer, By his rules I had to abide. The examples he tried to set, To my son I'll try to pass on. If only a few of these I met, Time is running out before he's gone.

They say, "apples don't fall far from the tree", The debt I owe him is a lot. His vision I'm trying to see. My father, my dad, MY POPS.

I know I'm coming full circle, Time with POPS is running out. And when he clears the last hurdle, I hope I don't sit and pout. His inspiration, his coaching, his stiff hand, Down on my knees to pray I'll bend. But in his honor, I'll gladly stand, For he's my father, my dad, my friend.

They say, "apples don't fall far from the tree", And from seeds you grow crops. I will try my best to carry on the legacy, He's my friend, my father, MY POPS.

PHATBOY Phil Marcha September 2022

The inspiration for this should be obvious. A great father figure John J. Marcha III was born in Green Springs Ohio

April 24, 1937, to two hard working parents. Strong work ethic was stressed in my raising. By the time I was 14, I had a full-time job pumping gas and would normally work 50 to 60 hours a week during the summer for a dollar an hour. We had a family of six and dad, at times, worked three jobs to make ends meet. As an Air Force family, we were far from rich, but we always had good food, clothes, and a roof over our heads provided by mom and dad doing the best they could. Hell, we didn't realize we were "white trash" poor even if we did have the newest and biggest trailer in the trailer park. We thought we were rich. My wife saw pictures of our early years in that trailer park, and she claimed that with our "White Pickett "fence and red roses, we had to be rich. Little did she know it was only about an 8-foot section that covered our small lot that our three-bedroom trailer sat on. The more I think about it, we were rich, and I attribute that to MY POPS!!

APPLES FROM THE TREE

While growing up, I never thought I'd say, "One day I 'll become a grandpa". Things my father said, I heard most every day. The wisdom in his words I finally saw.

I catch myself saying these things, I didn't think I could believe, Out of the fruit it brings , Simply APPLES FROM THE TREE.

The colors of the apples, Yellow, green, or red. It really makes no difference, With all the things he said.

If sooner I had listened, And took his words to heed. The lessons came to fruition, Understanding APPLES FROM THE TREE.

Sometimes it's been hard to admit, The things that came to be. Coming true from where I sit. Blinders made it hard to see.

Life lessons are often hard to accept. No denying what will be. Trust in your faith and here's the best. Families are built, APPLES FROM THE TREE.

So, when you're having doubts, And struggle with your decisions. Don't be scared to think about, Those that came before and their vision.

Their plan is sometimes hard to swallow, But brothers trust in me. We have no choice but to follow. For we came, APPLES FROM THE TREE.

PHATBOY Phil Marcha July 2022

I wrote this in July of 2022 sometime around my 62nd birthday. Trying to follow in my father's footsteps was a challenge as he set the bar so high. There are days, I must admit, that I don't know if I'll ever be half the man that my father is. At 87, he still outworks me and many others that are half his age. After retiring Chief Master Sergeant from the USAF, he became a general contractor. His work was meticulous, and his business very quickly became successful as "word of mouth" started generating around town of his dedication to finish jobs on time, his fair price, and doing what he said he would do. When he and his partner, another retired Chief, decided to retire from their business, he asked me if I had any interest in taking the business over. Now I have become a pretty good carpenter and to this day it's my hobby and stress relief, working with wood. But I had to pass on his offer as I didn't think I could do it 24/7 and more importantly, I didn't want to ruin his reputation which was impeccable. Food service was and is my passion and I think I got my skills from another "branch" of the family tree, my mother. She was a lot nicer and had more patience.

MAMA'S PAIN

I went to see her, On a cold and windy day. There was so much I wanted to tell her, But I just couldn't find the words to say.

She danced with the "invisible ghost", I know he thought he won, But what I wanted to say the most, Even after the damage was done.

MAMA'S PAIN, is part of HIS plan, MAMA'S PAIN will soon be done. MAMA'S PAIN was erased by HIS hand. MAMA'S PAIN won't go unsung.

From the day she brought me to this earth, The pain she endured was just the start. Who could imagine from by birth, How strong this woman, how big her heart.

Who would have known through living years, How many times have I caused her tears. The things I did and what I put her through. Can't be undone I know is true.

MAMA'S PAIN is part of HIS plan. MAMA'S PAIN has got me crying.

MAMA'S PAIN was erased by HIS hand. MAMA'S PAIN there's no denying.

I went to see her for the very last time. She had no idea who I was. Wish I could take her pain and make it mine, If only just because.

The pain she's in should be a sin, But my faith is in the man. He'll take her soon and it will be a win. I know it's part of HIS plan.

MAMA'S PAIN is hard to explain. MAMA'S PAIN I'm looking for closure. MAMA'S PAIN was not in vain. MAMA'S PAIN, by God's grace is finally over.

PHATBOY Phil Marcha February 2021

Inspiration, if you can call it that, was during COVID. Mom and Dad caught COVID Christmas of 2020. Dad survived. Mom unfortunately did not. She fought hard for six weeks but she had some underlying health issues. Recovering from an abdominal aneurism, a punctured heart, the beginnings of dementia, and a few other issues, she just didn't have the strength to beat COVID. A mother of four rotten, hellion boys, she was there for us constantly even when we put her through hell. When dad was flying missions to Vietnam in the late 60's, she was a very strong woman dealing with us four boys. Seems like we made a trip every week to the hospital for stitches, broken bones, getting my stomach pumped out of berries that I'd eaten etc. And there were trips to school to get my obstinate ass out of trouble for fighting or calling out people on the bus. It was extremely hard those last few days to see the fear in her eyes and not be able to tell her everything was going to be alright. I must admit that I prayed to God to take away MAMA'S PAIN. He finally gave her well-deserved angel wings on February 9th, 2021.

CRYIN' THIS COVID AWAY

I never thought it would happen to me, From this invisible enemy. A destructive foe I must admit. Thought with my strength, I could fight it. Can't pound nails with my father, Can't even hug my mother. Missed a reunion with my frat brothers. Too many people had to suffer. My wife, my son, my friends at bay, Wish I could CRY THIS COVID AWAY.

The tears have yet to dry. Beer and whiskey by my side. I sit, isolated, lonely, depressed. There's no reason to even get dressed. Faith and hope I try to keep. Many prayers before I sleep. Seems like I talk to HIM all day. Trying to CRY THIS COVID AWAY.

I know others in the same boat are hurtin There's one thing to know for certain. He'll find a way to grant me strength. Good health to return in short length. I pray that soon this will pass. Just be patient and at long last. And at the end of the day, I'll CRY THIS COVID AWAY.

PHATBOY Phil Marcha August 2020

The inspiration for this came at the height of the COVID scare we all went through. In my opinion it was the biggest lie ever told to not only the United States, but to the world. Now don't get me wrong as I later got COVID, and it was rough. When I wrote this, I didn't test positive even though I was exposed. The "hype" and not knowing if I did have it and not wanting my wife, my parents, my grandkids, or my fraternity brothers (our yearly reunion) to be exposed was quite stressful. Let alone if I could even survive it was quite concerning. The thoughts that were rolling around this big head of mine until I could get a test, well to be honest, the whiskey couldn't drown the tears. Watching TV for three days deepened my un-trust for our government and the media spin just about drove me crazy. My thoughts turned to the seniors in nursing homes being isolated from their families during their last days still pisses me off. The lies and misinformation that was being spread were flat out unacceptable. Think of all the tears, pain, lost business, social disfunction, and division COVID cost us. One day there will be a day of reckoning for this crime and for those responsible, I'll shed no more "tears".

WHAT'S GOING ON...AGAIN

Over 50 years ago, a young man wrote a song. The lyrics described things "Going" wrong. The social injustice, and police brutality. Half a century later, we're living in his reality. Add political corruption and abuse of power. Illegal immigration, and fake news every hour. Identity politics, war and people accepting sin. I must ask, "WHAT'S GOING ON AGAIN"?

You think we would have learned his message. And avoid this social wreckage. But no, we still live in such a mess. I honestly believe it's God's final test. How could things have gotten this bad? The division in this country is quite sad. You can be blind, and you can pretend. The question remains, "WHAT'S GOING ON...AGAIN"?

You would think in fifty years we would heal. Race issues gone, and we wouldn't feel. Things our ancestors did to create this debt. How we right the wrong, haven't figured it yet. I guess we just hit our knees at night to pray. For strength and guidance at the end of the day. And when we meet our "Maker" and trust in HIM. He'll a have the answer to "WHAT'S GOING ON.... AGAIN"?

PHATBOY Phil Marcha December 2023

The inspiration for this comes from one of my favorite songs by Marvin Gaye. Unfortunately, he left this world way too soon. My question is, how could a song that was written 50 years ago about the problems in our society still be happening today? Have we not learned? Was his message not heard? It blows me away how we, as a society, have regressed on these issues as we should be "Healing" from lessons learned.

Another favorite of mine that Marvin did was "Sexual Healing". I pray that someday we can find some "Racial Healing". But with today's media, both social and network, it seems we're headed down the wrong road and 'WHAT WE'VE BEEN THROUGH" for the last 4 to 5 years is horrible and irresponsible. The trust in our government on both sides of the isle is in my opinion, at an all-time low.

WHAT WE'VE BEEN THROUGH

It's been said, "What doesn't kill you makes you stronger". Hell, I don't know if I can stand this any longer. The stress, the mess, I can truly attest. Reaching my "Gloden Years", has been a test. My faith, my health, my respect for fellow man. My strength, "love for country", my future plan. Where we're heading I haven't a clue, One hell of a ride, WHAT WE'VE BEEN THROUGH.

It seems we live in a world of hate. Our actions will decide our eternal fate. "Love's In Need of Love Today". So, make some time to stop and pray. For he will be our "guiding light". To end this useless and silly fight. Each day, a choice to start anew. Let's put to bed WHAT WE'VE BEEN THROUGH.

WHAT WE'VE BEEN THROUGH can't be denied. WHAT WE'VE BEEN THROUGH, open our eyes. WHAT WE'VE BEEN THROUGH, it's been a test. WHAT WE'VE BEEN THROUGH, pray for the best.

What scares me the most about our future. Is education and influence, taught on computers Our social skills, lost on-line. How our children will be defined. The division we have between right and left. The price of groceries is hard to digest. All of the violence we watch on the tube, Lord please help us, with WHAT WE'VE BEEN THROUGH.

To coin a phrase, "The strong will survive", But when I look into my grandchildren's eyes. There's no telling what their future holds. Broken dreams from broken molds. At the end of the day, we must have faith. This fear that chills me, like a wrath. These questions haunt me, choices are few. God only knows, WHAT WE'VE BEEN THROUGH.

WHAT WE'VE BEEN THROUGH is so amazing. WHAT WE'VE BEEN THROUGH, much like hazing WHAT WE'VE BEEN THROUGH, we stood a test. WHAT WE'VE BEEN THROUGH, I pray we will be blessed.

PHATBOY Phil Marcha July 2023

During the last 5 years, I've been through a lot. The loss of my mother and brother, COVID, my health issues, the division of our country, the invasion at the border, the complete deterioration of trust in our government, retirement, I could go on and on and on. Turning 60 has definitely "Been a Bitch". I truly get up every day with tons of anxiety about what negative news will be reported and if I can even believe what's being reported. I've given up on trying to make a fortune just trying to protect what I have. Daily survival is my motivation, and I've hit the lottery with my surviving brain cancer. I've truly been blessed. Working at the prison for 2 years has changed me, for the better. My biggest fear is what this country has in store for my kids and grandchildren. I'm scared to death for their futures, so I dedicate my days to try and teach them some of my "street" knowledge and "old school" ways. My first restaurant boss (Tired Tom) from the first restaurant I worked at used to say all the time, "WHAT A COUNTRY". It's taken me 50 years to finally understand those words.

WHAT A COUNTRY

WHAT A COUNTRY we're living in. The corruption, division, the media spin. It's hard as hell to make it through the day, The lies, the attacks, with what they say. Marvin wrote "What's Going On" fifty years ago. The message in his song seems so apropos. When do we put this division to rest? When do we do for our children, what's best?

WHAT A COUNTRY we're living in. The corrupt stubborn elected is the biggest sin. Abuse of power seems to be the norm. Does faith in God help weather the storm? When do we hold their feet to the fire? The debt left to our grandchildren climbs higher. It doesn't matter if you're the left or right. No need for shades, for our future's not bright.

WHAT A COUNTRY we're living in. Wondering if we're just a bunch of has- beens. Do we have the strength to survive? Do we get IT back while I'm still alive? Do questions still remain unanswered? We need to hold ourselves to higher standards. We owe it to those who have come before. Let's end this division, let's stop the war.

WHAT A COUNTRY we're living in. I long for the day we will hear again. Crowds in unison chanting USA USA USA. And we're the envy of every child at play. For our freedoms are second to none. And we can honestly boast "we're number one". With these words heard from sea to shining sea" The United States of America WHAT A COUNTRY

PHATBOY Phil Marcha January 2023

The inspiration for this, as bad as I hate to say it, is the situation that our country is currently in. I was born in 1960, and I've never seen us so divided. You can point fingers and place blame, but I honestly feel like it's our own fault. We "buy in" to what the media is selling, bottom line. What we see and hear on TV and what we read on social media is killing us as a nation. There is no accountability in what is spewed out of the mouth of the anchors or hosts of every talk show or news or blogs or chat rooms. Disinformation, talking points, false accusations, outright lies and "fake news" runs rampant. There is little or no compromise from our elected officials and everything is based on what your political party beliefs or narratives are. Both sides of the isle are guilty of this. As you might of guessed I'm a conservative living in one of the most conservative states in the union. This is how I was raised, and my values are not going to change. My old boss, tired Tom, used to say, "I yam what I yam". As I said before, he would sit at the bar and watch the news with a "bullet" (Coors light can) in his hand, get disgusted with what was being reported, shake his head, and claim "WHAT A COUNTRY" …nuff said.

WE'RE HEADING TO CIVIL WAR

WE'RE HEADING TO CIVIL WAR. We're at the dividing door. The media has split this nation. What they spin is an Obama Nation. I've said it for several years. The path we're on is clear. I'm so tired of the fight for power. This day is not our finest hour. It's time to fight the fight. And stand for what is right. Does the hate for one man? Interfere with God's plan. "One nation" in "God we Trust". My friends, our government is a bust. It's true on both sides of the isle. They've missed "United" by a country mile. We need to fire them all. And once again stand tall. For our freedom is certainly at risk. Let's turn off the media blitz. And go have beers at the local bar. Before we end up in "CIVIL WAR".

PHATBOY Phil Marcha May 2024

Inspiration for this comes from the last few years and the "campaign" for POTUS. I've never seen so much hate for a candidate and so much support for someone who didn't, in my opinion, deserve to be a candidate. I truly don't understand how a candidate of a party doesn't get one delegate vote and is allowed to run for president. I can't remember any time in history that has happened. But I'm only 65. And the "hate" for another candidate came to a head with an assignation attempt. I thank God for "DIVINE INTERVENTION". Can I get an Amen from at least half of you readers?

DIVINE INTERVENTION

The date was July 13ᵗʰ 2024, Our country is on the brink of civil war. The summer heat was beating down. Thousands gathered in a Pennsylvania town. To hear a man talk, who millions feel hate. Who knew what would decide his fate. Just a few days before an important convention. Call it what you want, I call it DEVINE INTERVENTION.

An innocent life, by mistake was taken, A shooters stray bullets, had the crowd shaken. A few others were hit, and for them I prayed. With God's grace they would be ok. A mixed up 20-year-old pulled the trigger. Consumed hate for the man, is all I can figure. The country being divided I won't fail to mention, We desperately needed some DEVINE INTERVENTION.

It was Sunday morning when I wrote this ditty. To those haters, I still feel pity. This man has been beaten, but never gave in. He's an extension of the ONE that forgives sin. It's an example of strength, this man displayed. Fight fight fight his message at the end of the day I'm calling on you, to help ease the tension. And pray pray pray, for God's DEVINE INTERVENTION

PHATBOY Phil Marcha July 14ᵗʰ, 2024

I wrote this after watching on TV live the assassination attempt of President Trump. Now listen to me when I say even though I'm a strong conservative, I'm not the biggest Trump fan. In 2016 my choice for the GOP nomination was Dr. Ben Carson. In 2024 my choice was Ron DeSantis. I'd explain my reasons but that's for another time. Bottom line is I believe Trump's first term; his administration had a lot of policy successes. You can't deny that. But his demeanor is lacking "Presidential "appeal, to say the least. Even after all the court cases and lawsuits and all the negativity spewed by the media, Trump not only won the popular vote but also but also the Electoral College 312 to 226 which in these days is considered a landslide. It's yet to be determined if on that fateful day DEVINE INTERVENTION plays out. We will see.

A TIME TO HEAL

What we've been through for the last 8 years. It has caused a few fights, and a lot of tears. We have some fences; we need to mend. Let's get down on our tired knees to bend. We've been horrible to our fellow man. Let's pray #47, has a solid plan. Put our differences aside, I hope you will feel. What I'm saying, it's A TIME TO HEAL.

I almost lost hope, but now I will trust. And pray that his promises won't be a bust. God has a reason for everything. His "DEVINE INTERVENTION" healing to bring. Stop looking back for the water has passed. Let's heal together, get rid of our masks. I'll do my part and here's the deal. Just give it a chance, it's a TIME TO HEAL.

I know it sounds corny, all these cliches, But there absolutely has to be a better way. Things have been said, and we've heard the lies. Red ones, blue ones, we all can't deny. If this country's success has a chance in Hell. For our kids and grandkids, believe my sell. Send up some prayers before your next meal. For it's not too late, It's A TIME TO HEAL!!

PHATBOY Phil Marcha November 6, 2024

I wrote this the day after American voters elected Trump as the 47th president of these United States. Not only did he win the popular vote, but he won all the swing states. Now I'm not going to get into the reasons why I think he won, to avoid argument, but there's no arguing that it was a mandate and I believe the people spoke loud and clear. Now is the time for him to prove out. And it's A TIME TO HEAL. Can you give it the chance?

2 B KNOWN 4

I have a question that we need to explore, What is the reason we are even here for? What's our purpose, what does He have in store What do you want, 2 B KNOWN 4?

Accomplishments? What is truly yours? Just own it, so no one can ignore. Have you made your mark? Or is there more? What do you want, 2 B Known 4?

It's a true test when you're standing at a door. Do you open it up? Do you dare risk anymore? Spread your wings and be ready to soar. The winds will change what you'll B KNOWN 4.

Chase your dreams maybe settle a score. But keep your feet firmly planted on the floor. Be true to yourself and expose your core. Accept the results for what you'll B KNOWN 4.

Represent your name, what you should strive for Honor your legacy of those that came before. Look in the mirror your true colors are your décor And just accept what you want 2 B KNOWN 4.

PHATBOY Phil Marcha March 2024

The inspiration for this writing comes from my wife, April. About a year ago, her employer, Lone Wolf Family Farms, a medical marijuana facility, decided to move the entire operation. The facility was on 15 acres in a rural isolated area just across from the lake that we live on. They moved to Tulsa Oklahoma, hello culture shock. Their business had grown so much that they decided to move the "grow" to a metropolitan area to accommodate the demand for their product. April was directly responsible for the growth and demand for LWFF. Since their move they have picked up many high-profile clients. Obviously moving to a major market, and her "pre rolls" being voted Top Five in the state of Oklahoma, the move is paying huge dividends. Now April was born and raised in a very small town in SW Oklahoma and had never lived "Big City" life. Tulsa is about 250 miles and a four-hour drive away from where we live. So obviously she and her son and her son's fiancé' had to move to keep their employment. It's an understatement that their lives had to change from living at the "lake" to living the fast-paced life of 800,000 people. To make matters worse the facility is "Downtown". As in every big city in America, the "Downtown" areas are quite different and dangerous and represent many daily challenges. Coming from a place where we don't lock our vehicles or doors and know firsthand all our 12 neighbors was quite the transition and adjustment. All in all, the move has been quite successful, and they are on a "roll" and further expansion is inevitable. I'm extremely proud of her for stepping through that door to follow her career and will continue to support her for it's her 2 B KNOWN 4 time in life. Her recent promotion to facility manager has her answering hundreds of questions and I feel like she finally understands. And it was her "CHOICE".

CHOICES

Some good, some bad. A lifetime of CHOICES I've had. With age should come wisdom. Mistakes? I damn sure made some. Every choice comes with a debt. Payment for some, I've not met yet. But I stand behind them wrong or right. For my honor, it is worth the fight.

Sometimes it's hard to choose. Hard to accept when you lose. Keep in mind he forgives your sin. Even if your CHOICES create a win. At the expense of just a few. Because they will make CHOICES too. Even if things don't go your way. Own them at the end of day.

The key to making your CHOICES soar. Is to learn from those who came before. Listen to your mom and dad. It was their CHOICE the reason you were had. And give some respect to your elders. Listen to their boring lectures. Shut your mouth and open up eyes and ears. Your CHOICES will be solid for years.

It's hard to tell the future. CHOICES made just might go smoother. When you learn from your mistakes. And understand there are no retakes. Give your CHOICES some serious thought. By the life lessons that you were taught. Have true faith in His guiding light. Whether your CHOICES turn out wrong or right.

PHATBOY Phil Marcha July 2023

Inspiration for CHOICES came from a lifetime of making some of the worst CHOICES one could make. As I explained before, growing up in a small town and in a military family, well let's just say CHOICES were few and far between. The repercussions of making the wrong ones held stiff penalties with not much tolerance. Living in the "straight and narrow" was the standard. My senior year in high school seemed like all I did was work. My parents wanted me, upon graduation, to attend the local junior college. My family was far from poor, but mom and dad could barely afford books and tuition at my CHOICE, the University of Oklahoma. This meant I had to pay for room and board and all the extra circulars (beer, car payments, beer, insurance, dating …did I mention beer?) while attending OU. So, in my senior year and the summer of '78 I worked and worked and worked. It was the only way to get out of this "one horse town". Even when I landed in Norman, OK in the fall, I worked a full-time job flipping eggs and burgers while juggling 15 hours, fraternity, beer drinking and socializing. Being away from home meant making my own decisions and CHOICES. Now to say there was a difference with living at home under the watchful eye of an ex-Sergeant and being on your own at 18, well let me tell you that the "schoolin" I got from making my own CHOICES and having to be responsible for the outcomes was more difficult than I could ever imagine. I was now experiencing "Life in the Fastlane" and I had the "pedal to the medal" and didn't take my foot off the gas til I was in my late 30's. Even then I drove in the left lane and didn't let anyone pass me until I hit 55. By then I had made so many wrong CHOICES and let's just say I'm still paying the "fines of life". Now at 65 I have no problem

letting people pass and occasionally even hit the "shoulder".
But those were my CHOICES, and I own every last one.

MY BACK YARD

Precious moments, fond memories. We planted grass, we planted trees. Tennis balls, my dog would fetch. With my best friend, we played some catch. Wiffle ball games we would play until dark. Those were great times in MY BACK YARD.

Easter egg hunts, the family cook -outs. The pickup games, the brotherly bouts. Fireworks in the sky, on the 4th of July. Simple star gazing and looking at the skies. The simplest of things, when times were hard. Good times were had, in MY BACK YARD.

With each move, the yards got bigger. Family of my own, I had to deliver. Memories for my kids were important to me. The plastic pools, pitching tents under the trees. The birthday parties, the games of cards. Many great memories, in MY BACK YARD.

I have grandkids of my own now, I live on a lake. Boating and fishing, more memories to make. The sun rises and sun sets, are second to none. The circle is closing, it's been a great run. Truth be known; I've been blessed by God. I hope they will plant me in MY BACK YARD.

PHATBOY Phil Marcha October 2023

My formidable years were obviously in the 60's and 70's. In the 60's we grew up in a trailer park in New Egypt ,New Jersey. Our trailer sat on a small lot on the edge of a forest. There was an estate home "way back" in the forest. At least once a week we would make the "journey" deep into the forest. Our goal was to make it to the fence that surrounded the estate mansion.

Armed with our stick guns we carried out our "mission" emulating the Vietnam War that we saw nightly on the news in the late 60's. Rumor had it that the gardener had a shot gun and had "buck shot" for intruders. Success was had when we touched the fence and immediately turned and ran back to our "hood" without getting "buck shot" in our little butts. One day we "hung" one of the kids we played with copying what we saw on either "The Rifleman" or "Bonanza". Thank God a parent saw what we were attempting and save our buddy. Restriction from playing in the woods followed. In the summer of '69 we moved to Oklahoma and mom and dad bought our first brick home on the last street in a new addition. We planted grass and trees in the "Red Dirt" that Oklahoma is famous for. Now this "brick house" was a just a 3-bedroom 1100 square home, but we thought we had our first "mansion". Dad soon poured a 12' by 12' concrete pad and put up a basketball goal. Man, we were in "Hog Heaven" The pick-up games and "Horse" games and cookouts and picnics began. When grass finally grew, then came the all day wiffle ball games and "smear the queer" football games. Great times and great memories. We moved across the cotton field in the summer of '76 and dad planted 2 pecan trees which he now harvests and makes great pecan pies. Mom had her dream garden filled with roses, daffodils, azaleas, ivy's, a magnolia tree and anything that would flower. Plus, a full vegetable garden that the squirrels from dad's pecan trees would ravage. Now MY BACK YARD is butted up to Hick's Mountain that is adjacent to Lake Lugert and I've definitely "moved on up".

HAD EM ON 8-TRACK

It was in the late 70's and the music was hot. Times were rockin' with the 8-tracks we bought. Our 6x9's blaring when we "ran the drag". All the memories of the good times we had. These bands were born, fame was their desire. Journey, Boston, Chicago, Earth Wind and Fire. Starting with the Beatles, it was "Getting Back". These iconic bands, I HAD 'EM ON 8-TRACK.

Of course there are single artists. They dreamt of climbing the chart lists. Back then there were just a few "Genres". At the time, we "might" have smoked marijuana. Jimi Hendrix had some "Purple Haze". "In Paradise" Collins sang "Just Another Day ". AC/DC did "Hells Bells" and "Back in Black". These music icons, we "HAD 'EM ON 8-TRACK".

We shouldn't take away from the artists of today. But the best music was" back in the day". The Eagles had a great song "Hotel California". Marvin "What's Going On" tried to warn ya. The Isley's did "Between the Sheets". Gap Band funked, "You Dropped a Bomb on Me".

Heatwave's "Always and Forever" will bring you back. To the days when we, "HAD 'EM ON 8-TRACK".

Although it was just a brief period in time. To not honor the 8-track, would be a crime. Face to Face with Billy Joel and Elton John. Led Zeppelin, Dylan, and Stevie Wonder songs. Ol' Hag and Willie, George's Strait and Jones. The 8-track era artists, I now have on I-phone. Those were the "Days my Friends" and looking back. It was the best of times, when we "HAD 'EM ON 8-TRACK".

PHATBOY Phil Marcha November 2023

The inspiration for this poem is self-evident. Rolling Stone and Billboard magazines both agree that the best decade of music was from '60 to '70. I tend to agree. The early to mid '80's came close in 2nd. A lot of these bands and artists from this era are still touring and still selling out venues and arenas all over the world. I still have my original 8-track player and two cases of 8-tracks that I bought when I had an extra $5. I'm in the process of writing another book titled "HAD 'EM ON 8-TRACK". It is quite a bit more in depth than this poem. The book is about the bands and artists from this era, where they are now, the history of how they got started, the break-ups, the reunions, the struggles, the alcohol and drug use etc. The research is quite extensive and interesting and time consuming. Hopefully it will be coming to a bookstore near you and Amazon soon. So, for now "Rock On" and "JUMP up and down in your BLUE SUEDE SHOES" and we'll have "FUN FUN FUN" til your Daddy takes the T-Bird away" and "Life in the Fastlane" will surely make you lose your mind!!! Ok I'll stop, cuz we could do this "ALL NIGHT LONG".

WHAT'S HAPPENED TO COUNTRY MUSIC

Lord, WHAT'S HAPPENED TO COUNTRY MUSIC? Has it died and gone away? All the pop, rap lyrics and 808 beats, Is all the DJ's play. Ol' Hank songs, Hag and George Strait songs, We hardly hear no more. It's hard to find twin fiddles playing, When I buy from the iTunes store.

Lord WHAT'S HAPPENED TO COUNTRY MUSIC? The hard times the artists sang about. Mama, old dogs, cheating and beer drinking, They all seem to get left out. What are these young artists thinking? I'd Love to hear a song, about work all day long. Sod busters working the land. Women that done you wrong. And not a Red Solo cup in each hand.

Lord WHAT'S HAPPENED TO COUNTRY MUSIC? Is it just a thing of the past? When do the lyrics of a song. Become iconic words that will last. Let's keep these things in mind. Good foundations we are searching to find. WHAT'S HAPPENED TO COUNTRY MUSIC I say, Has it died and gone away?

PHATBOY Phil Marcha March 2024

The inspiration for this writing is the ever-changing music and lyrics in the Country & Western music genre. Now I understand "crossovers" are an integral part of the music industry but I'm a traditionalist. I must admit I didn't listen to much C&W growing up. I think the first real C&W artists that I liked were Merle Haggard and Glen Campbell and Steve Wariner. Then came Alabama, Restless Heart, Diamond Rio, Rascal Flats and I finally enjoyed the "King" George Strait's music. Now I know the bands that I mentioned had a little bit of crossover flair but when Alan Jackson and George Strait song "Murder on Music Row" hit the charts, I finally understood. But I guess if the Cody Johnson and Laney Wilsons are still putting out good country music, I can live with WHAT'S HAPPENED TO COUNTRY MUSIC.

P.S. Beyonce winning the grammy for best Album and best Country Album is indicative of this. What a joke!!

MISSING MY REASTLESS HEART

It all began in 1984. "Til I loved you", knocked me to the floor. There were "Wheels" "Blue Eyes" and "Cries". "Big Dreams", "Fast Movin Trains" and some "Tender Lies". These three "Okies" a Kentuckian and a Yankee. "Wrong or Right" it was destined to be. There were hard times and "Fences to Mend". They became "Long Lost Friends".

They had "Julliard" talent and great harmonies. "Don't Ask the Reasons Why", they were family. In "New York" they "Held Her Tight". Their cover of "Wichita Lineman" was spot on right. Many a wedding heard "I'll Still Be Loving You", The" Eyes of Texas" were colored "Blue". Their music captured and climbed the charts. Man, I'm MISSING MY RESTLESS HEART.

From stadiums, dive bars, and rodeo arenas. I couldn't wait to see them. My son's favorite "That Wok Won't Row", These boys were damn sure "On a Roll". Their fame and fortune were made real soon. Even on 8-track I had their tunes. "Iron Horses" & "Fast Trains" was just the start. Can't deny I'm MISSING MY RESTLESS HEART.

"Still Restless" , "Big Dreams" in this small town I hope my writings will someday be found. "Down the Road" I hope I'll find my "Miracle", And "Looking Back" I'll reach my poem pinnacle. For my "Grandbabies Need New Shoes" for sure. Here's to wanting some success "And More" I'll close with I loved their music from the start. Damn I miss, RESTLESS HEART!!

The inspiration for this is the "Inspiring" music of RESTLESS HEART. Truly one of the greatest Country/Pop bands since the Eagles. My "Smalltown" favorite son Paul Gregg left Altus Oklahoma to follow his "Big" dream in Nashville. In the early 80's while I was running Graham Central Station, the biggest C&W night club in OKC at the time, Restless Heart came to play. The club was packed and they "killed" it. Their music mirrored the music of Alabama, and everyone loved them. Now I have to say that three of them were from Oklahoma, but I don't think that mattered much. They were damn good and on the path for nominations from the Academy of Country Music for top vocal group. Every year from 1987 to 1991 they were nominated and won the award in 1990. They finally got recognized by demoing "Love in the First Degree", written by Tim DuBois for Alabama. It was Alabama's first crossover hit and peaked at #15 on Billboard's Hot 100 in 1982. That collaboration put the band "Okie Project" on the path to becoming Restless Heart and the rest is history. One of my personal favorites "Don't Ask the Reason Why" was a collaboration with David Foster on the soundtrack of "Secret of my Success". Love that song. They recently covered Glen Campbell's "Wichita Lineman" and featured their great harmonies and musicianship. Man, I definitely miss their great music, and I consider them in my Top Ten bands of all time. "That's my story and I'm stststicking to it"!!!

STANDING IN THE CIRCLE

In music comes many setbacks. Chasing the "Dream" you must stay on track. Few make it to the top of the hill. But on the journey, you experience some thrills. From dive bars to stadiums and big arenas. In hopes that thousands will come to see ya. You will know that you've jumped the last hurdle. When planting your feet STANDING IN THE CIRCLE.

I know it's just part of an old wooden floor. Where many have planted their feet before. Many dues you must pay to get there. Sometimes you're just "Living on a Prayer". Even when you have given your best. Often times you will fail the test. The steps you take seem as slow as a turtle. The reward is surely STANDING IN THECIRCLE".

There are many worthy venues. Red Rocks and the Ryman to name a few. The Fillmore, MSG, Royal Albert and the Greek. But there ain;t no better place to land your feet. Many have stood in this famous place. Jitters and anxiety they had to embrace. For some it took years to clear the last hurdle. They got a chance STANDING IN THE CIRCLE.

The list is long, growing from year one. Ol' Hag and Jones, Willie and Stapleton. Dolly, Loreta, Miranda, and Crow. Alabama, Restless Heart and even Jelly Roll. The list is long, and some passed too quickly. Patsy, Presley, Lefty and Whitley. If you stood there, you'd become Immortal. Can't take it away, STANDING IN THE CIRCLE.

The older I get, appreciation for many things, But mostly for what, great music brings. And who knows what the future holds? For those that dream their music goes gold. There's a stage in Nashville, Tennessee. This historic floor is at the

GRAND OLE OPRY. Yes, you can say, membership is fraternal. Once you make it, STANDING IN THE CIRCLE.

PHATBOY Phil Marcha March 2022

The inspiration for this is truly my love for music. Being from a musical family and not having as much talent as my brothers had, my only hope is to write something worthy enough for someone to put to music and a song. Just call me Bernie looking for an Elton as I lack enough music theory to formulate a melody. I ran a Graham Central Station on 2nd street in Nashville that was four stories and had a "rooftop" stage looking over the Cumberland River. The "A" team, and the best studio musicians would come play that stage every weekend. Grahams was located between BB Kings and The Wildhorse. Of course, I took part in many adult beverages at the live music bars that lined Broadway. In addition, I worked concert security while in college and then worked for a tribe in Oklahoma that had five casinos and a 2000-person event center. Needless to say, I've seen many artists and bands from every genre. I could write a book on the bands and artists "riders" and what I've seen backstage and on their tour buses. But that's for another time as I'd have to retain a very good lawyer to be able to tell what I've witnessed. I'll just keep writing in hopes that someone will see my lyrics worthy of a song. I doubt that I'll ever "STAND IN THE CIRCLE" , but two of my closest fraternity brothers who played in the "Pride of Oklahoma" marching band and had the opportunity to "STAND IN THE CIRCLE". Stranger things have happened.

TUFF LOVE

It's been said "Love's in need of Love today". Agreeing, I'd be remiss if I didn't say. There are all kinds of Love, this is true. "Crazy Love", "Puppy Love" and love that made you blue. "Love Hurts" and sometimes it's unbearable. "Love thy Neighbor" straight out of the Bible. "Lasting Love" is represented by the dove. But allow me please, to talk about "TUFF LOVE".

"TUFF LOVE" seems to be a thing of the past. But will these "Lessons in Love" truly last? There's "Endless Love" and "Love Gone Wrong". "Bad Love" , "Faded Love", all great songs. My "Vision of Love" was taught by my mother. Dad taught "TUFF LOVE" to me and my brothers. It's the little things the stiff hand out of the glove. "That's the Way Love Goes" is sent from above.

"Bleeding Love" & "I Want to Know What Love Is" "Unconditional Love" is a message of HIS. The message of "TUFF LOVE" often not learned, But the "Best of my Love" has to be earned. Going through "TUFF" times, walk hand in hand. Realize that "The Power of Love" is in HIS plan. When you're "Looking for Love" look to the skies. Your prayers will be answered "TUFF LOVE" does not lie.

PHATBOY Phil Marcha December 2023

The inspiration for this comes from a Stevie Wonder single "Love's in Need of Love Today". This single is off one of the greatest double albums ever recorded, Songs in The Key of Life. This album eventually went Diamond and is considered by Rolling Stone Magazine in the top 5 albums ever. It had a place in Phatboy's top 5 8 -tracks case. You already know how

I feel about Marvin Gaye's "What's Going On" and the lyrics from Stevie's song "Hates going round breaking many hearts, stop it please before it goes too far" resonates my feelings with what's happening in our society today. Both of these iconic songs seem apropos almost 50 years later. It's evident in today's parting words "Love Ya" when saying goodbye to not only family, but with lifelong friends. We need more of this but not only saying it but showing it. I'm not so sure we've made it that far, yet. But it's a start. The "Tuff Love" my parents showed is the ultimate example. And I'm glad it was taught in my family.

JELLY ROLL TEARS

Music is one of my passions. And it ain't about fashion. It's about what cuts deep, In my heart that I try to keep. The songs that move me the most, Often I take the time to toast, When enjoying a few cold beers, Songs that bring JELLY ROLL TEARS.

It could be when your dog died. Or even when momma tried. It could be when you've lost, A good friend and you bared the cost. You think your world has come to an end. On bent knees with prayers, you send. Just wash away your fears. And cry ya' some JELLY ROLL TEARS.

We all go through things in life, And yes they can cut like a knife. The songs that pull at your heart, Sometimes you need a fresh start. With music it soothes your soul, Whether it's country, blues or rock and roll. Songs that forever linger in your ears. Once you've cried some JELLY ROLL TEARS.

Ol' Jelly is a sensitive big man. He's proof that God has a plan. Remember "You can't unlive where you're from" Don't leave your dreams undone. You better believe his tears are for real. For his true fans, it shows true appeal. His cries are met with cheers. The honesty of JELLY ROLL TEARS.

PHATBOY Phil Marcha October 2023

The inspiration for this was discovering JELLY ROLL more than five years ago. I was surfing You Tube for SIMPLE MAN, and I came across Shine Down's cover of the Lynard Skynyrd's classic. They invited JELLY ROLL, who was backstage, to sing the song with them on stage. Now this song is truly one of my favorites and will be sung at my funeral. I was mesmerized and hooked. The next video of JELLY was with Craig Morgan singing "Almost Home" at the Grand Ole Opry. Man, I cry every time I watch this video. Soon came "Long Haired Son of a Sinner" and the rest is history. I was working at the prison, and I researched his back story and influenced my band orderlies and other prisoners to check him out. His success was very inspirational with them and JELLY is doing great work with real reform not only with drug rehab but knowing that there's life and opportunities for these guys when they get out. For me, everything he writes hits home, especially his latest "I AM NOT OKAY" "UNPRETTY" and "WHAT'S WRONG WITH ME". The lyric "Standing on a bridge I'm burning with a can of gasoline" from the song "HALFWAY TO HELL" or the message from "CHURCH" …..Man I've been there done that. When my wife and I went to Sturgis in 2024 we had planned to see him at the Buffalo Chip, but it was sold out. We cried some JELLY ROLL TEARS. But we stayed at the campground, and we had our own little concert playing his music while drinking beers and having shots of Fireball and Crown Apple. I encourage anyone struggling with drugs or alcohol to discover him and purchase his music. His message of "God is real and all things are possible" with tears rolling down his face…..spot on!

WHISKEY DRINKIN' AND SOME DEEP THINKIN'

I 've finally come of age, Hopefully able to turn the next page. In these writings about my life. I dedicate this to my wife. We've had our ups and downs. I love me some You Tube sounds. I'm trying to bust some rhymes. While we're missing some quality times. Just: WHISKEY DRINKIN' AND SOME DEEP THINKIN'

Where do we go from here? Don't worry, just grab another beer. Let the MAN lay out our plan. And with faith trust in His hand. I know these times are tuff. And yes, I miss you, Sho Nuff!! But let's give thanks to what we got. The test of time will prove out. Still: WHISKEY DRINKIN' AND SOME DEEP THINKIN'

This "test" is meant to prove. If our love is really true. Many couples have been down this lonely road. Life in the fast lane has surely slowed. While others have had their doubts. This opportunity will prove out. I'm damn sure in this to the end. With my prayers to Him I'll send.

Done: WHISKEY DRINKIN' AND SOME DEEP THINKIN'

PHATBOY Phil Marcha August 2024

The inspiration for this came about six months after my wife, April, moved to Tulsa for her job. It was soon after we had returned home after Sturgis. We bought a Minnie Winnie 24' travel trailer and pulled that "thang" to Sturgis S.D. and back. Yes, I was officially a retired senior citizen. It was not quite a year after I had a full knee replacement, we made this trip. It was definitely a learning experience. I had never pulled a trailer of this size over 2000 miles round trip. When we got back and she went back to work in Tulsa, stress relief and decompression were in order. So, WHISKEY DRINKIN' AND SOME DEEP THINKIN' were born. All in all, it was a good trip, except for missing Jelly at the "Chip", the 2000 miles was very stressful, but the whiskey made my belly "full"!!

JUST AN OLD COWBOY….AT HEART

I'm no Rip, no Gus, Captain Call or John Wayne. Never been with a herd on an Oklahoma range. I can count on one hand when I rode a horse. Never won a buckle at a rodeo, of course. Wore ropers and wranglers just to look the part. I guess I'm JUST AND OLD COWBOY…AT HEART.

Love George Strait songs, been a two-stepper. My scratch country gravy, load up the pepper. Many a mile "On a Steel Horse I Ride". But I'll go to war with my brothers by my side. It still remains, in cowboy ways I'm not smart. Still, I'm JUST AN OLD COWBOY…AT HEART.

Now "out west" to the mountains I've ridden. Been fishing and hunting and things forbidden. Live in Oklahoma, many Texas towns I've been. Love me some sunsets, but my skin is not thin. Never branded a calf, not too late to start. Truth be known; I'm JUST AN OLD COWBOY… AT HEART.

My word and honor, with a hand shake I'll give. Through wind and rain and tornados I've lived. A few bar fights, and lots of whiskey I've drank. I've never broken ice from a frozen water tank.

Someday soon from this world I'll depart. Let it be said Ol' Phatboy was JUST AN OLD COWBOY…AT HEART.

PHATBOY Phil Marcha February 2024

Being born at McGuire AFB/Fort Dix, New Jersey in the summer of 1960, who knew we were going to move to Oklahoma in the summer of '69? But that's where the Air Force sent us. The first 9 years of my life were spent on the east coast. I remember the Jersey shore, lots of trees, and damn good seafood. I'd never seen a cow or a horse or a Native Indian. That all changed when we moved to this "God Forsaken" state as did many other military families in the late 60's. We were in culture shock. The next few years, not only did we see cows, horses, and Indians, but also Mexicans, buffalo, elk, deer, jack rabbits, skunks, armadillos, tarantulas, "horned toads", crawdads, catfish, mountain lions, rattle snakes, red dirt, tumble weeds, and yes, tornados. We saw fist-sized hail, 50 mph winds, lightning with snow, black ice, and in the spring, temperatures in the teens and the next week temperatures in the 80's and 90's. We ate "chicken fried" steak and white country gravy, okra, black eyed peas, chili with no beans, fried catfish, enchiladas and tamales, and even on occasion, fried rattlesnake. Now if that ain't country," I'll kiss your #@ss". In high school, I sported over-all's and in college, boots, wrangler jeans and starched button-down shirts was the dress. Now I looked the part and even was mistaken as "Garth Brooks" one time while driving my pick-up truck and wearing my "black felt" Resistol hat. I never got into AG, FFA, or rodeo. When I saw my first rodeo at the age of 12 or 13, I knew right there and then that I wanted no part of bulls, steers, heading and healing or dipping. Hell, I didn't even learn to appreciate country music until I was close to 30 years old. After college I went to work for the biggest nightclub in OKC, Graham Central Station, that was in the early 80's. Back then, the NFR was in OKC and every December, we were the place to be. These were pre-Urban Cowboy days and I learned two-steppin', ten-steppin' , and waltzing. "Line Dancing" was born but I'm proud to say I've never "line danced". We had a huge dance floor and when you put 200 cowgirls in "Rockies" on the floor line-dancing, well I did appreciate the "view". After managing the OKC club I got transferred to Arlington and Fort Worth Texas to manage a couple of clubs, and later Amarillo. Austin, and Nashville on 2nd and Broadway. Needless to say, I got "edumacated" on country music, country women and good clean country living. At this same time my little brother Scott was touring with this guy named Toby Kieth and I could relate with "Should Have Been a Cowboy". Some of my favorite movies and series are obviously the Clint Eastwood spaghetti westerns, Deadwood, Yellowstone and my all-time favorite "Lonesome Dove". With all this said I'm nowhere near a true cowboy but......I'll be dammed if I'm not.... JUST AN OLD COWBOY...AT HEART!!!

AIN'T NO FENCE BUILT AROUND ME

I've gotten old and tired; it seems like overnight. What this world has become is just not right. Yet to be determined, what my legacy will be, Know this…AIN'T NO FENCE BUILT AROUND ME.

I used to be bullet proof; I could go all night. Wasn't scared of no one, never ran from a fight. My resolve has not changed, it will be what it be. Believe this, AIN'T NO FENCE BUILT AROUND ME.

The way things are, sometimes out of control. I was taught by my father; I've accepted my role. To stand with strength and defend my family. You "betta" know, AIN'T NO FENCE BUILT AROUND ME.

There will come a day I won't be at my best. But rest assured, I'll put up a strong test. Just knowing I'm a branch from the family tree. Be prepared, AIN'T NO FENCE BUILT AROUND ME.

No trash talking here, no bragging no boast. I'll sit down with you with beers to make a toast. Not looking for trouble or to make an enemy. Trust me, my friend, AIN'T NO FENCE BUILT AROUND ME!!!

PHATBOY Phil Marcha March 2023

The inspiration for this comes from a sports radio host from The Sports Animal in OKC. My good friend ,Willie T with whom I worked with at Graham Central Station back in the 80's works with this "host" and accuses me of being a twin of this "host". What a Yardbird!! Just because I'm right 95% of the time about sports in general, doesn't mean I'm this guy's double. Now I will admit this "host" is a conservative alpha who speaks his mind and rarely takes any s#@t from his callers and stirs the pot on occasion. Any talk show host will do the same from time to time to create controversy making for good radio. Many times, the "back and forth" conversations get a bit heated and when callers call him out his normal response is "Come get some you yardbird sissy boy, there AIN'T NO FENCE BUILT AROUND ME". I admit I've had a few confrontations similar to this with my life-long friend Willie T, but it's all good fun. We normally make up over a few shots of BLUE SOCK!!!

OL' BLUE SOCK

In the wonderful world of whiskey. Some of the "rot guts" you partake of is risky. There's bourbons ryes and blends. They're aged to let you know when. Just like with some fine wines. Good whiskey gets better with time. It's been said Chevy trucks are "Like a Rock". Just give me some OL' BLUE SOCK.

For some they like the lites. And tequila has caused some fights. There are all kinds of Jamaican rums. Consumed on Islands you'll have some fun. Flavored vodkas there are way too many. Cold beers, trust me, I've had plenty. I've yet to acquire the taste of scotch. I'll just stick with OL' BLUE SOCK.

Now there's Apple, Peach, Blackberry and Black. Quite trendy, and that's a fact. It takes at least 12 years to age. It's Royal in every way. But for me I'm glad I found. From Canada this whiskey called Crown. Drank with a mix, straight up or on the rocks. I've drank my Phil of OL' BLUE SOCK!!

PHATBOY Phil Marcha July 18, 2023

The inspiration for this simply put, I love me some Crown Royal. I started bartending at 20 years old when I was attending the University of Oklahoma. I lied on my application as you had to be 21 years old in Oklahoma. I started cooking at Tom's It's About Time at 16. This was a bar/restaurant, so I learned quite a bit about BLUE SOCK before I actually consumed it. My first bartending job was at Spurs in OKC. Now 80% of our sales where "long neck" bottles of Coors Light, Budweiser, and Miller Lite. It was 1980 and that was your choice. The whiskeys that were available was Crown Royal, Jack Daniels and Jim Beam. The Law was 18 for beer and 21 for liquor. In the early 80's, in Oklahoma, there was finally a transition in 1983 that you had to be 21 to drink any form of alcohol. During these years it was a distribution nightmare and Crown Royal was not distributed in Oklahoma. When Crown was on the hiatus during these years, another Canadian blend called Merit replaced Crown as the taste profile was similar. Merit came in a Red cloth bag as opposed to Crown that came in a purple/blue cloth bag. After about a year, Crown returned to Oklahoma and the Oil business was booming. So, an "Oily" came in one night and bellied up to the bar and ordered a "BLUE SOCK" and coke. Well, I had never heard of BLUE SOCK before, and I politely said we didn't have that. He said sure you do "think about it". I couldn't put 2 & 2 together and he finally told me Crown and Coke. Duh…. the light bulb went off. Of course, now there's Green, Peach, Brown and Black "Socks" but my "sock drawer" is predominately "BLUE"….Git Er Dun!!!!

YOU CAN'T OUTRUN YOUR RASING

It's been said, "You can run but you can't hide". Someday when we get to the other side. He knows everything you've done in your past. You won't be able to hide behind your mask. So, stop looking back and move ahead. You can't unsay the things you've said. Wake up and avoid the time you're wasting. Realize, YOU CAN'T OUTRUN YOUR RAISING.

Some things I've done, I'm not really proud. I'm guilty of running with the wrong crowd. "Water's run under the bridge" a great analogy. I pray my actions have not affected my legacy. With each new day, chances are given. To make a change to the way you're livin'. It gets harder with the challenges we're facing. Know this, YOU CAN'T OUTRUN YOUR RAISING.

Lessons learned from your family tree. Passed down from generations, I'll guarantee. From your father's father & your mother's mother. The name they built, you should rediscover. Teach these things to your kids and grandkids. Lessons of love, leave nothing hid. On my gravestone, I hope they'll be engraving. That I didn't… OUTRUN MY RASING.

PHATBOY Phil Marcha October 2024

Inspiration for this came in a couple ways. The first is a Jelly Roll (with Yelawolf) song Unlive with the lyrics "You can't Unlive where you're from". I was discussing this song with my frat bro and best man who stood side by side with me in my first wedding. He comes from a similar background as me but from a town that is roughly 1/6 the size of my hometown Altus (19,000). He grew up in a town of roughly 3000 and has done very well for himself including at least 6 oval office visits. I've ridden with him in Sturgis and still talk politics with him from time to time as he is definitely "in the know". He's a man of faith and pray I can match his "faith" and his words, YOU CAN'T OUTRUN YOUR RAISING.

G-PA

Seems like it happened over night. The "lay of the land" doesn't seem right. But the best thing that ever happened to me. My son gave me a present to continue my legacy. I've not aged well and it's not fair. And yes, I've lost most of my hair. But the thing that puts me in awe. Is from my children's children, the title G-PA.

Seems it was yesterday; I thought I was young. Still living in the fast lane and having fun. Now my focus is to protect their future. And with honor, become their ultimate teacher. To try and connect with love teach them right. It's against all odds; but with strength I will fight. I'm trying my best, don't need a hurrah. The reward is knowing, I'm their G-PA.

I know I don't have a lot of time left. But I'll be damned if I don't give it my best. The goal is for them to accept my family's legacy Let them know "Apples don't fall far from the tree". It takes some tolerance to accept what they do. And to fend off the troubles, they'll get into. I'll try to teach them, the meaning of God's law. And try to be the most honorable G_PA… of all!

PHATBOY Phil Marcha July 2024

The inspiration for this is simply the responsibility of being a grandfather. To pass on to my grandchildren what has been passed down to me is my mission, plain and simple. To have the opportunity to teach and mentor my grandkids every day is a responsibility that I don't take lightly and welcome the challenges to make a difference in their lives. If I can teach them the lessons that my grandfather's taught me and keep them from making the mistake that I made…. well, that will be my greatest success.

MY BROTHERS

What started in the Fall of '78, Turned out to be, something truly great. A journey of well over 40 years. There's been lots of laughter, been a few tears .

From boys to men, this poem I send. This special bond we share I will defend. To my "brothers from different mothers". It is admired by many others.

We faced adversity, we passed the test. Pride for OUr University, when I'm laid to rest. The moments I remember, some things I regret. It's "Not over til' its over", more fun you can bet.

When we get together, the stories that we tell. Some things sacred and could land us in Hell. And as the years go by, one thing is a fact. All MY BROTHERS, know I have your back.

We have a special bond that's shared by few. Years of camaraderie that we made it through. Thankful for the good times had with the "Boys". When we get together, we talk a lot of noise.

So as I close, there once was a prose, By the younger PiKA's. I love all MY BROTHERS to hell with the others, "I'm glad I'm not.... (but I Yam) …..Phil Marcha".

PHATBOY Phil Marcha #1287 July 2023

Inspiration for this has come from my initiation into Pi Kappa Alpha (Beta Omicron) at the University of Oklahoma in 1978. This lifetime experience was and still is a huge part of my life. Now truly, the events my brothers and I went through were some of the best times of my life. And some of these times could have landed us behind bars, yet some of the shenanigans we experienced in bars. All in all, I wouldn't trade these five years of my life with MY BROTHERS in college or the years after, for anything. And I'd be remiss to my "boys" at GCS if I didn't include them as MY BROTHERS. Still to this day there's not a week that goes by that I don't converse with MY BROTHERS either by texts or calls or emails. The banter is still "alive and kicking" and we share a couple of reunions every year. The beer and "Blue Sock" get to flowing and the stories, the lies, the memories, the embellishments, and the real truth comes out and its quite entertaining to say the least. And yes, some of these stories and memories will remain between….me and MY BROTHERS!!!!

BRO HOS

What started back in '78, Who knew what would be OUr fate. What would become of us, who could know. Our future label, BRO HOS.

We decided to join a Frat... Years later, OUr hosts became TY and Rat. We all came from different folds. One brother's wife coined us BRO HOS.

We've been through thick and thin. This group committed many a sin. Our first trip we went to Mexico. Close to 50 years later we became BRO HOS.

We are all brothers, from different mothers. Years later, for OUr actions there is no cover. The times we've shared where fun "Fo Sho", Within this prose, to be called BRO HOS.

OUr yearly reunions have been a blast. Don't know how much longer it will last. In the sand we'll dig in OUr toes. And stand tall and proud to be called BRO HOS.

PHATBOY Phil Marcha September 2024

The inspiration for BRO HOS came from the stories of the reunions I've experienced at Lake Eufaula in Oklahoma and OUr fraternity Founders Day every year on or around March 1st. A couple of my frat BROS have very nice lake homes at Lake Eufaula. They are gracious enough to host a reunion every year. In addition, my fraternity has a founders day celebration every year and we all get together and relive OUr past over some adult beverages. Well one of my pledge brothers, who I spent a few hours in a Nuervo Laredo Mexico jail with, and will remain unmentioned, his wife, after years of hearing the stories of OUr past coined us BRO HOS. How fitting?

KINDER & GENTLER

After years of hard living, I hope some will be forgiving. For a time in my life, My words and actions cut like a knife. I just thought I was pretty bad, As a middle child a strong father I had. My mother gave birth to four boys. Every day was a fight and lots of noise.

Striving to be KINDER & GENTLER

Growing up at times was a struggle. My family wasn't the type to snuggle. Every day there was a competition. We got used to this kind of livin". We had respect and "unspoken" love. And we prayed to the MAN above. Sibling rivalry seemed to be the norm. I thank God we weathered the storm.

Working on KINDER & GENTLER

Getting older has softened me. At times I get down on bended knee. Throw up thanks for being blessed. Because He's granted me forgiveness. I haven't changed that much. But I admit that I've been touched. By His hand He's leading me. A "Better Man" my promise to be.

Praying to become KINDER & GENTLER

PHATBOY Phil Marcha October 2024

The inspiration for this has come with post brain surgery. Something happened to me when I had that tumor removed a couple of years back. Now some say I had some "meanness" cut out of my brain. I won't argue. Something has definitely made me KINDER & GENTLER. Maybe it's because I've retired and no longer have the stress of running a business, financial worries, losing my mother and a brother, or not having to answer a hundred questions a day (love you babe), but I've certainly mellowed. I've learned to NOT let the little things in life stress me out. I've also learned that I can't control everything and to just let the Man upstairs "take the reins" and have faith and trust in Him. Man, that was a hard lesson to learn. Thank you, Pastor Paul, I couldn't have done it without your guidance. You put me on the path of becoming KINDER & GENTLER and I'm forever grateful.

READY TO RETIRE

Been a working man well over 50 years. Have shed a little blood sweat and tears. Put a few miles on this body of mine. Starting to realize, "It's About Time". This old flame is losing its fire. I'm thinking I'm READY TO RETIRE.

Ain't made no fortune, but I've paid my way. I'm proud of my work, at the end of the day. There's a lot to be said for the things I've done. It hasn't been easy, but its damn sure been fun. My body is spent, seems like "I'm so tired". Not much left in the tank, I'm READY TO RETIRE.

I've had a hard life, and life's not fair. Unlike G Jones, I'm ready for the rocking chair. The places I've been, the people I've met. It's been a good run; on this you can bet. The stories I could tell, I won't be a liar. "No Future in the Past" I'm READY TO RETIRE.

I have been fortunate, these places I've been. I've seen blessings and I've seen sin. I've done things most men can only dream. Regrets you ask. Only a few and far between. Just once or twice I've tripped on the wire. The question remains, am I READY TO RETIRE?

I know where I've been, not sure where I'm going. The hard part to face is the not knowing. I must have faith in the days that lay ahead. "Coming Full Circle" you know it's been said. I'll trust HIM to rekindle my fire. And I'll question my thinking, am I READY TO RETIRE???

PHATBOY Phil Marcha June 2023

When I wrote this, there was another "lockdown" at the prison. I had just received a suspension without pay for leaving my office with my computer still logged on to the internet. Now I was not issued a radio as was SOP and it was the two o'clock count and as normal, I had to secure my gate to the Gym yard. The trouble was I had left my two most trusted orderlies in the office with the internet on my computer. We had been listening to and watching You Tube videos, and I failed to "log off". Well two Cos (correctional officers) who came to the Gym to secure movement for lock down noticed that I had left the computer on, and the two orderlies had "access" to the internet. When I received the suspension, I asked if in fact either one of the inmate orderlies actually got on and when we ran surveillance video it proved that neither had touched the computer nor gained access to the internet based on the history of the computer. So, in short, leaving my office for five minutes it took me to secure the gate. It cost me a three-day suspension without pay. I had already put in for leave prior so what was a 7-day leave turned into a 10 day leave which meant 10 days without recreation for the prisoners. Who were they punishing? When I returned to work the prison was on "lockdown" and once again I found myself alone in the quiet Gym and I had time to reflect on the situation and began asking myself, do I really need this chit? My job is to provide recreation for 1000 inmates in the form of athletic activities, music and band, hobby craft, leather craft, games on the units and some sort of semblance of life beyond the walls of stone and bars of steel and I get suspended? For trying to do it right? Well, "rules is rules". I took my suspension and immediately filed for medical leave to have my knee replaced. When the doctor released me early, I might add, I demanded a meeting with my supervisor, the head of HR and the warden. The intent of this meeting was to address my position and to make a decision whether or not to return to work. I had had many issues with the Deputy Warden and it was her decision to suspend me. In addition, I had many issues with her, but I won't get into them. Well, the day of the meeting I limp to the head of HR's office with a well-planned written agenda to discuss my further employment. My supervisor, the HR head and the Deputy Warden show up. About 1/3 of my agenda had to deal with specific issues that I had with her and her performance. After about two hours of "negotiation" and her promising the moon, I made the decision to return to work. This was late October. I resigned my position in the middle of December as her promises failed to come to fruition. By then I was READY TO RETIRE…..so I did.

THE GARAGE PARTY

It's Friday night in the big town. A bunch of old farts 'bout to get down. We've been friends for many years. We shared many laughs; we've shed a few tears. By sundown whiskey and beer get to flowin', We have no idea where it's all goin'. We tell some jokes, some occasional malarkey. A bit of "Old School" fun at THE GARAGE PARTY!!

We come for fellowship, play our favorite tunes. Hell, even sometimes we howl at the moon. We share old memories; we share some smoke. Very rarely is a harsh word spoke. For years we've shared each other's company. Sometimes we break bread it's "on the money". We share a common thread; we all ride Harley. A bunch of seniors chopping it up, at THE GARAGE PARTY!!

With the time we have left, the days are few. Our friendship is solid, our friendship is true. The man upstairs has blessed us for sure. And what we have you can rest assured. That many people go through the years. Living in doubt, living in anger, living in fear. Until we meet again, my friends, don't be tardy. Can't wait until the next, GARAGE PARTY!!

PHATBOY Phil Marcha November 2024

The inspiration for this comes from my biker friends and you know who you are. But may I say that most bikers are good people. April and I used to do a "Toy Run" every December and what we found is most bikers are big givers. Not only in "Toy Runs", but bikers are the most charitable blue-collar people I've ever met. "Poker" runs happen every weekend when it's nice enough to ride and most of these events are linked with some kind of charity. The events bikers go to every year raise millions of dollars and MC's (motorcycle clubs) for the most part have good intentions. I'm an independent biker which means I don't affiliate or wear "colors". And most senior bikers don't. We just enjoy our freedoms and don't have to impress anyone. We enjoy "Fellowship" and laughter and an occasional adult beverage. And what's so wrong wit dat?

YOU MATTER TO ME

Sometimes things are left unsaid. As we try to move ahead. The daily grind passes us by. We're lost in the fast lane, and we wonder why. The hands of time will soon erase, Precious moments we shared and faced. But there's one thing I can guarantee, Brothers and sisters YOU MATTER TO ME.

You see we started as just friends. On your character, I came to trust and depend. With your consistent friendship, rest assured. The years that passed became a blur. But with each day that passes us by, I wonder then ask the reasons why. Our true friendship came to be. To put it simply, YOU MATTER TO ME.

Our days together will soon run out. And our fellowship sadly we'll go without. Some great memories will be all we have left. Our departures will leave me quite upset. But soon our reunion will come to fruition, And once again I'll make it my mission.

To let you know the reasons to be, Why my friends, YOU MATTER TO ME.

PHATBOY Phil Marcha September 2023

The inspiration for YOU MATTER TO ME came from one of my fraternity brothers, BROTHER BOOM. While traveling for a visit with Pastor Paul I received a call from Brother Boom. After the normal chit chat, I asked the reason for his call and he politely said, "Because YOU MATTER TO ME". He confided that he had been reading trying to improve himself and his duty as a grandfather. Now Brother Boom has 13 grandchildren and is kept busy trying to be the best Grandfather he can. Brother Boom and I are on opposite sides of the fence when it comes to politics. Through the years we have definitely had some quite heated debates on our views. But he's "old school" conservative democrat and I can live with that. Recently with the last election, he told me he was concerned that the outcome, if it happened, would affect his job and position of being a Democrat. Well, it happened. I don't know if he knows this or not but if the "shit hit the fan" and I pray it doesn't, I'd stand side by side with him to protect his family and I believe he would do the same for me. Why you ask would a Republican defend a Democrat in this day and age? Simple, Brother Boom YOU MATTER TO ME!!!

ACKNOWLEDGMENTS

I have so many people to thank for inspiring me to write this project.

TO MY PARENTS: Thank you for supporting my endeavors and me. To Mom up in heaven, I miss you every day. Your approval for my first writing COMING FULL CIRCLE inspired me to continue writing. To Dad, thank you for building with Mom, a loving home built on structure and discipline. Yes, we had some disfunction, but most families do. We didn't have a lot, but we had enough. Sometimes that's all it takes to make a "Home".

TO MY WIFE APRIL: Thank you for your support and feedback. There's an old Three Dog Night song "Pieces of April" and I sure got "some". Some good, some bad, but all in all I could not have done this book without you. Your feedback has inspired me. And BTW, thank you for teaching me how to drive. I must say you are my favorite "little driver helper" but can you avoid the turtles, racoons, coyotes, deer, and rocks…. please?

TO PASTOR PAUL: You have no idea how you have helped me with my "faith" and helped me understand that God has a plan and purpose of us all. I'm learning to "give up the reins" more and more and trust in His "Inspiration" and recognize His blessings. I pray for your continued health and admire your strength. I know that every day is a challenge for you but with God's grace, you somehow make it happen. Love you, Bro!!!

TO MY FRATERNITY BROTHERS and you know who you are. Man, what we went through as pledges and finally brothers, the memories and stories have definitely given me "inspirations" for this project. To those of you who sent the first draft copies of my writings, thank you for your feedback. But most importantly, thank you for tolerating me and forgiving me for some of the things I did to you. My intentions were to build character and create memories, some good and yes, some bad. Please grant me "forgiveness". Phi Phi KA!!

BETA OMICRON PI KAPPA ALPHA

This thing started at the University of Virginia, The legacy here at Oklahoma will continue. The hard work and dedication of many, The guarantees of success are plenty.

When I first pledged, we were rollin. We had no idea that soon we'd be foldin. Full of pride, we became brothers, We went on "walk outs", like no other.

Through the years, we may have fallen. But like the BAD A's, we still be ballin'. Thanks to perseverance, and strong will. We've overcame and climbed the hill.

So, on this Founders Day, I must give thanks, To those of you who served in the ranks. Representation of those in OUr bond, I'm damn proud of this thing we've spawned.

So, in closing, we have traveled from afar, And later, let's toast at the bar. To celebrate this special Founders Day, Here's to you, the men of PiKA.

Phil Marcha class of '78 #1287

TO MY TEACHERS: especially my Jr. High English teachers and my Speech teachers. Your tolerance and "paddle" guidance were definitely "Inspirational". I finally understand the value of good grammar and comp. Had I been born 40 years later, I would not have needed y'all for things like spell check, editor and all the other writing tools that computers have. But I thank you all the same. "I be just kiddin'"!!!

TO MR. AND MRS. WIG, You probably don't realize, or maybe you do, how special you are to me. Thank you for your words of encouragement and your "Red" pen. I could not have accomplished these writings without your honest critiques and feedback. I love you both!!

TO MY FRIENDS AND FAMILY and co-workers, ex-employees, bosses (well, some of my bosses), and a special shout out to my orderlies at the prison, I sincerely thank you. Watching over and working with you "on the daily" was truly a lifetime experience. I hope I have had a positive influence on you. Stay strong and keep your heads held high and commit to being "better men" by trying to do right. And as always stay "Prayed Up".

It's been said that everlasting friends go long periods of time without speaking and yet never question the friendship. These friends pick up like they just spoke yesterday, regardless of how long it has been or how far away they live, and they don't hold grudges. They understand life gets busy but there is always love there.

Attitude to Inspiration